UNDER THE WHITE ENSIGN

UNDER THE
WHITE
ENSIGN

D. J. Maslin

The Book Guild Ltd.
Sussex, England

*To Mary who
kicked me into
writing it*

This book is sold subject to the condition that it shall not, by way of trade or otherwise, be lent, re-sold, hired out, photocopied or held in any retrieval system or otherwise circulated without the publisher's prior consent in any form of binding or cover other than that in which this is published and without a similar condition including this condition being imposed on the subsequent purchaser.

The Book Guild Ltd.
25 High Street,
Lewes, Sussex

First published 1993
© D. J. Maslin 1993
Set in Baskerville
Typesetting by Southern Reproductions (Sussex)
East Grinstead, Sussex
Printed in Great Britain by
Antony Rowe Ltd.
Chippenham, Wiltshire.

A catalogue record for this book is
available from the British Library

ISBN 0 86332 813 X

CONTENTS

List of Illustrations   6

Chapter 1	*The War, 1939-1945*	7
	About the Eastern Med. 1940-1942	9
	About the Atlantic 1942-1943	21
	1943-1946: The Eastern Med. Again	25
Chapter 2	*Aftermath and Peaceful Pursuit, 1946-1952*	34
Chapter 3	*The Far East, 1952-1955*	46
Chapter 4	*Far East Aftermath, 1955-1958*	69
Chapter 5	*The Home/Med., 1958-1961*	73
Chapter 6	*Epilogue*	86

LIST OF ILLUSTRATIONS

The author, then an Engine room Petty Officer, 1944   28

The author as a member of the Home Fleet
Boxing Team, 1949-50   36

HMS *Implacable* at anchor in Villefranche, 1950   38

HMS *Comus,* Okinawa, 1954   51

The surviving members of the HMS *Comus*
football team, 35 years on, at their reunion
in Portsmouth, 1991   52

HMS *Armada,* 1958-60, during Cyprus campaign   73

1

The War
1939-1945

Great oaks from little acorns grow. No truer saying exists; where would the great oaks come from, other than little acorns? But I wonder how many ocean-going careers begin on cross-channel ferries, from our shores. From such modest beginnings began my naval career. I suppose it was inevitable anyway. My father was a long serving naval man, and I had an uncle in the Merchant Navy. Water on the brain you might say.

'Twas early in 1939, with war clouds gathering over Europe, that I decided to take a holiday in Jersey. My workmates in London could not understand my choice. What's the matter with Southend? What's the matter with Brighton? Why go all that way? Jersey was thought of as some far-flung outpost of the empire. With the exception of the more elderly staff who had served in the 1914-1918 war and had seen France briefly, no one had been anywhere other than Southend or Brighton for holidays. How the world has expanded.

The previous year I had spent my holidays in Ilfracombe, North Devon, all alone, aged sixteen. That was lunacy enough, thought my friends, but Jersey, across the sea was considered as a trip to the moon would be today.

Southampton to St Helier, that's where it all began.

I returned from this intrepid journeying in June 1939, and almost immediately applied to join the Royal Navy. Examinations followed, at the recruiting office in Wimbledon and in Whitehall, and I was in. Or was I? With the gathering war clouds, reservists were being called to the colours, and were clogging up barracks and depots. New recruits were cut to a trickle until ships were found for the reservists. So I was sent back home to await the call. Waiting was purgatory; how could they possibly enter a war situation without me? It was not long in coming, but I remember it seemed interminable.

Basic training (and it was basic at this time, cut down drastically due to circumstances) was soon complete. You were taught just sufficient to get you sea-borne, and that was it; the rest of training was carried out at sea. Mine was done in Portsmouth and Gosport. Portsmouth was my depot and remained my spiritual home for the next twenty-two years. Over that period there were times when I loved it, times when I hated it, but looking back now, it wasn't a bad old dump.

My training class were a cosmopolitan lot, to say the least, from all walks of life. But only myself and one other made it to the end of the road, out of about forty. We never crossed paths during the intervening years, but did meet up on the day we retired, twenty-two years to the day, in 1961. Approximately half never made it to 1945, all summoned to the big ship in the sky.

There were four coal miners in the class, three Geordies and a Taffy, all having joined up to escape the grind of pit life. The Taffy was the one who completed the journey. The three others found a back door out of the Navy; yes, you have guessed it, back to the pits.

About 1942, the country was so short of miners to produce the coal needed for the war effort that they offered any ex-miners a free discharge from the Forces provided they went back to mining. So one must assume that life in the pits was preferable to life at sea. Or did life expectancy come into it? I don't know.

But back to 1939, as continuation of the training process I spent the next month or so on a series of ships in Portsmouth for brief periods, among them the aircraft carrier *Ark Royal* and two old V and W class destroyers *Velox* and *Vortigern*. All three were subsequently sunk at various stages of the slaughter to come.

Then off to war. I did not see the United Kingdom again until 1942. My draft was to HMS *Resource*, supposedly in Freetown, Sierra Leone, at the time. I took a passage from

Liverpool on M/V *Abosso* of the Elder Dempster line, with regular runs to West Africa. A banana boat really with a small passenger-carrying capacity.

The only port of call was Dakar, Senegal: my first foreign port I suppose.

By chance, travelling on *Abosso* to West Africa happened to be a prominent Merseyside boxing promoter, and whilst at Dakar he decided to run a tournament; Navy v Merchant Navy. A ring was rigged over one of *Abosso's* hatches, and it proved quite successful. I was the Navy's welter-weight, and a mate was chosen at middle-weight, a lad from Wolverhampton.

I must say my spirits dropped when I discovered who my Merchant Navy opponent was to be – a 'name' professional from Liverpool. Above my class. No chance, I thought to myself, and when my Wolverhampton mate suggested we pool our purse money, I jumped at the idea. The purse money incidentally was £2 per winner, £1.10s. per loser. Laughable now, but I remember our pay at that time was 17s. 6d. per week, so it represented over two week's pay.

Come the event, my opponent won the first round well, having me down once; but in the second round I caught him with a good right hand which shook him. Encouraged by this I poured it all on, and knocked him out late in the second. Elated? Of course I was. But! And here comes the rub, my middle-weight friend lost!

We arrived at Freetown to discover the *Resource* had left, weeks previously. After a few days, passage was arranged back north to Gibraltar on the cruiser HMS *Neptune*. Eventually after a stop in Bathurst (now Banjoul) and Casablanca we arrived in Gibraltar and joined the *Resource*.

Our ultimate destination was Alexandria, to join the strong Anglo/French fleet that was assembling there ready to combat the Italian entry into the war, which was becoming more inevitable as day succeeded day. We did have a short stop in Malta en-route.

ABOUT THE EASTERN MED. 1940-1942

What can I say about this period? Disaster followed disaster, defeat followed defeat. I suppose the first blow fell with the capitulation of France to the Germans. The French fleet in Alexandria was in turmoil; half wanted to return to their homeland and face ignominy, the other half wanted to continue the war on the Allied side. Eventually a compromise was arived at. We certainly could not countenance the French ships falling into German hands, but allowed the crew members that elected to do so to return to France; the rest just sat out the war in Egypt. But the important thing was their ships were immobilized.

It was touch and go. Both fleets nearly finished up on the bottom. We were in Alexandria the night that the two fleets trained their guns on one another. The situation was one of the most explosive of the war. Potentially explosive that is, and thank God it remained that way. Diplomacy eventually prevailed. Had it not, the result does not bear thinking about. Both sides had battleships with fifteen inch guns and in the close confines of Alexandria harbour the carnage that would have resulted can only be imagined; not only to the two fleets, but a large part of the city would have suffered as well.

So at a stroke the naval force in the Eastern Med. was cut by half. At about the same time the enemy force was increased by about sixty per cent with Italy's entry into the war.

I served on a number of ships about this time. Although I belonged to *Resource*, smaller ships would come in after being in action, with dead and wounded, and their crews would be temporarily augmented by crew from larger ships. A few less on a big ship would not be missed, but to a smaller ship each man was vital. *Carlisle* and *Calcutta* were two that come to mind that I had spells on.

North Africa was a tale of woe in its entirety at this period. As the enemy advanced and (occasionally) retreated, we saw action along most of this coast, from Algeria to Egypt, mostly in support of the army, supplying them from time to time as large units would be cut off. Tobruk was a classic example. I don't know how many times it changed hands, but when it was 'ours' it had to be sustained by sea. Stopping the enemy from supplying its army was a never ending and increasingly hopeless task.

Air power was the ace card the Germans had over us. Their air bases in Southern Italy and North Africa attacked us relentlessly. Our air power? Well it just did not exist. Even today I could not tell a Spitfire from a Hurricane. How could I? I never saw either. But a Stuka! I had nightmares over those things. They literally poured out of the skies at us, unopposed.

The campaign in Greece added further to our desperate situation. We were doing well in the Western Desert at the time, when half our land forces had to be diverted in an effort to save Greece. Result? Further disaster on two fronts instead of one. The Greek campaign had to be mounted and succoured by the navy. Then as Greece fell, the land forces had to be evacuated on to Crete, only to fall very shortly after. Our losses were horrific in these battles. On one day alone we lost two cruisers and four destroyers – *Fiji, Gloucester, Kashmir, Kelly, Greyhound* and *Juno*. All from air attack.

At one of our airports on Crete, near Chania, there were ten or twelve RAF planes, fuelled and armed, which had to be destroyed, blown up; there were no crews to fly them. When we asked the army what had happened to the crews, we were told, 'Oh they went back to Egypt weeks ago'. I understand that the C in C, Royal Air Force, Middle East, was sacked after the Crete debacle.

This is a subject I could go on about, really go on about. But I tend to get bitter. So the subject is closed. But I must say in closing it that things did improve after this.

A few words are appropriate here about the Greeks. They fought valiantly. When the Italians first invaded Greece from Albania the Greeks were hammering them; it was only on German intervention from the north that they buckled and we had to go in to assist them. But it was too little, too late. Their navy did get away, most of it to Egypt, and fought on; but most of their ships were old, ex-RN and Italian.

They really appreciated our help and that appreciation has continued. On visits to Greece in 1959 and 1978 and Crete in 1980 I was made very welcome, even more so when it was revealed that I had been in those battles. In fact in a little village on the Peloponese I had a taste of being a local hero. All those years later, reflected glory. But that is a story in itself, not appropriate here.

The foregoing remarks about the Greeks also apply to the Yugoslavians in my opinion. They loved their country and fought for it.

Sport and recreation were not high on our agenda at this time, as can be imagined, but both were taken in Alexandria as opportunity presented itself. There just wasn't anywhere else; Malta was besieged, Palestine (Israel) was visited occasionally. The enemy controlled the rest of the Eastern Med. We really were backed into a corner.

One day I was about my work on board when out of the blue I got what was known as a 'pier head jump'. Briefly that is a draft from one ship to another at a moment's notice. Not so bad when both ships are in the same harbour, but mine was in Alexandria and my new one was supposedly in Ismailia. It rejoiced in the name of HMS *Hopper 33,* a minesweeper. Its (I refer to it as 'it' without much affection) previous and original destiny was as a Suez Canal Co. mud hopper. As the canal was dredged, the dredgings were transferred to a hopper for disposal into deeper water. Our living quarters were once the mud area. Shocked? Yes, so was I on arrival. The navy had converted them into minesweepers.

But just getting to it was quite a saga. I was taken to the railway station, a ticket to Ismailia was put into my hand, and I was left with kit bag, hammock and rifle. 'Royal Egyptian Railways'! The cynicism which the inverted commas infers is not unintentional. I was well aware that had I taken my eyes off any of my three items of luggage for more than a few seconds, I would never have seen them again. I have encountered some adept 'tea leaves' in my world-wide travels, but never any as adept as the Egyptians.

Fortunately for me, on embarking the train I teamed up with some soldiers returning to Cairo after a few days leave in Alexandria. So we took it in turns to nod off during the night, safe in the knowledge that our belongings were being kept an eye on. This liaison had another effect on my journey; thank goodness for those soldiers. They told me that this train went to Cairo, and nowhere near Ismailia, and that I must change trains at Benha. Had I not met them, guess I would still be on a train heading south.

Benha was a rail junction off the Alexandria/Cairo line to Ismailia and Port Said. Just a small station, with a cluster of wattle and daub houses adjacent to it. I left the train at dawn and my heart sank a little, I must admit. I could not find out the time of my connection because of language difficulties, and in fact I stood there for about five hours in the desert sun in full uniform, not daring to take my eyes from my treasured possessions. Thankfully my train eventually arrived and I got to Ismailia. There was an army transport office there and they contacted the navy communications station for me. I then stood on Ismailia station for another two hours before being collected.

Bear in mind that I had not eaten or drunk for over twenty-four hours by now, and in that climate! On arrival I was told that the *Hopper* was not in, and would not be until the following day. I was taken somewhere to spend the night in an Egyptian 'hotel'. Once more inverted commas and implied cynicism. But at least I had a bed, plus food and drink.

It was nearly midnight by now, but worse was to come. I never did get into that bed. A jeep full of redcaps pulled up, found me, and conveyed the glad tidings that the *Hopper* had just come in and I was to join her straight away as she was sailing again in the morning. Up goods and chattels, into the jeep, down to a jetty. They dumped me there in pitch blackness, saying, 'There is the *Hopper*,' and off they went. When my eyes adjusted to the light, there was the *Hopper*, indeed. Out in the middle of Lake Timsah. I was on the jetty, not a soul in sight or sound. I tried hailing, but to no avail, she was too far out.

Eventually I paid a felluca which happened to pass to take me out. It was 0200 by this time and fifty hours since leaving *Resource*.

On arrival I was greeted with, 'Oh yes, we are sailing at 0600 and you have the morning watch', which for the uninitiated commences at 0400. The hoppers were all coal fired and there I was at 0400, shovelling coal.

Some days in one's life are best forgotten, but one can tell by the preceding few paragraphs that I have not forgotten them, probably never will. I was a teenager at the time, which could have been an advantage I suppose. I had lots of resilience.

The Germans at this time were dropping mines into the Suez Canal, mainly magnetic and acoustic type, the objective being to sink shipping and thereby block the canal. They did sink a few ships but never did succeed in blocking the canal totally. The hopper's job was to 'sweep' these mines almost as they were dropped. Observers would tell us where they fell (must say this information was not always reliable) and we would 'pulse' over them until they blew. Accordingly our regular routine was Port Said, Ismailia, Port Tewfik, Ismailia, Port Said, then more of the same.

We would leave Port Said, firing furnaces from the plates, shovelling upwards; now the normal practice would be to ditch ashes over the side daily, but no way, that was currency! By the time we returned to Port Said, we would be standing on about four feet of ashes, firing downwards. Then no sooner were we alongside, than an Egyptian contractor arrived. He bore the unlikely monica of Jim Irish. An Egyptian named Jim Irish! Well one needed a bit of humour in those grim days. A price was negotiated for the ashes and they were promptly removed.

This used to supplement our rations. On these small ships a system operated called canteen messing, whereby the Admiralty paid us so much per day to victual ourselves. This was an iniquitous system, so the extra cash was most useful; it enabled us to sustain a reasonable standard of victualling.

Once again crews could be switched around as the situation demanded, I had a spell on the *Hopper 39*. This went on until the *39* was sunk off Fort Kabrit. I had a more organized trip back to Alexandria this time round, to the base camp at Sidi Bishr, to await another ship.

It wasn't long in coming either, HMS *Naiad*, a cruiser of the Dido class, pretty small by today's cruiser standards. In fact it was smaller than the destroyers of today. The Eastern Med fleet had by this time been reduced to about three of these cruisers and about ten destroyers. In fact we were flagship, an unprecedented occurrence. Rear Admiral Vian, whose wartime exploits are well documented, was the 'boss'.

All our battleships were gone by now. The *Barham* I remember going down and the last two, *Queen Elizabeth* and *Valiant*, were sunk in Alexandria harbour by Italian men in miniature submarines. A very brave attack from their point of view. From our viewpoint, one more disaster to add to all the others.

I can sum up my time on *Naiad* in one word – 'Action!' You were in action from the time you left harbour till the time you returned. You were hammered twenty-four hours a day from above, with the occasional U-boat action as well.

It all came to a horrible climax on March 11, 1942. The action started with a Fleet Air Arm plane hitting an Italian cruiser somewhere north of Malta. She was last seen heading slowly for Taranto. The fleet, such as it was, was dispatched from Alexandria to intercept and sink her. I, along with a lot of others, was ashore that evening enjoying the odd bottle of Stella, when military police vehicles toured the city, rounding up crews of all available ships. A general recall, it was known as. We sailed during the night, full speed for southern Italian waters.

We were still a long way from the crippled cruiser when we received Fleet Air Arm information that she was going to reach Taranto long before we could get there. So the whole operation was changed.

There happened to be, at this time, one of our cruisers holed up in Malta. She had been hit by bombs, some time previously, and had limped into Grand Harbour. She had been repaired sufficiently to make her seaworthy and had made a number of unsuccessful attempts to get out and back to Alexandria. Well, there we were, not too far from there and available, our original mission having been aborted. We broke radio silence and told her to crash out and join us to come under our protection. Needless to say, the moment we broke that radio silence, all hell broke loose. Every surface ship, submarine and aircraft at the enemy's disposal was hurled at us. How could they not risk everything for such a prize? The total remnants of the Eastern Med. fleet set up ready to be shot at. Once again, no air cover!

Well, our cruiser, I can't think of her name after all this time, joined us and we headed back to Egypt. Every second of every minute of every hour of that next twenty-four hours we were hammered. By this time I had been on the receiving end of some hammerings, but this was the worst. The fact that we came through that barrage without loss can be attributed to fortune favouring the brave.

That night, the third of the operation, as we progressed eastwards, the intensity of the attacks diminished and late evening we relaxed; one watch was relieved from action stations to eat. I was one of that watch and it was the first time we had eaten for around thirty-six hours. That food tasted good, and the conversation was of being back in Alexandria the next day and a run ashore. We were pretty well out of enemy aircraft range at this time. Only surface action to worry about.

A naive statement that, if ever there was one. At around 2000, disaster struck. A U-boat had lain directly in our path, engines stopped so that we did not pick her up, and from close range she fired a torpedo into our starboard side. It hit us right on the bulkhead between A engine room and B boiler room, thereby doubling the amount of initial water intake. We took nearly thirty minutes to sink. The list was immediately to starboard and a number of fires broke out on that side so no lifeboats were launched from there at all. The boats on the port side, as they were launched, fouled the ship's side, due to the list. So with a couple of exceptions, the only life saving equipment available were floats. I must emphasize there was no panic. I was below and had to come up through two decks and was carried along on a tide of humanity. We were listing badly by now.

I went over the side and swam away as quickly as possible, before someone else jumped on top of me. It was pitch black. I got away about fifty yards, then trod water in order to blow up my life belt. You wore one from the moment you left harbour till the moment you returned, in a deflated condition, so it was just a matter of inflating it. I felt happier in a way once it was inflated; a sort of 'I'm alright Jack' feeling came over me and I swam gently away from the stricken vessel with conservation of energy in mind. Such complacency was exposed when after, well I don't know how long, I touched my life belt to find it completely deflated. All the tests that had been carried out at set periods over the previous years had been to no avail. To say my heart sank is the understatement of a lifetime.

I was still close enough to the ship to hear her death throes. She went down by the bows; the stern rose out of the water and I could quite clearly hear the screams and anguished cries of men trapped, and of men in the water with the hull coming down to engulf them. Those cries linger in my memory yet and will never leave me. I don't have nightmares over it, but the memories will never leave me as long as I live. We lost ninety-two men. Life (or death if you like) is strange isn't it? One of those lost was a mess mate of mine. He was a superb swimmer, a navy water polo player, in fact more at home in the water than the average shark. I watched him enter the water well ahead of me and swim away easily and confidently. Now I am an average swimmer to say the least. He died and I lived. Fate?

I swam away in the blackness and came across one of our Carley floats with several men aboard, and joined them with a sigh of relief! But as the night progressed we were joined by more and yet more men until the float began to be dragged underwater by the sheer weight of humanity. We made some adjustments, allowing the injured to come 'inside' the float whilst the rest of us hung to the ropes on the outside. Even so, the thing was still sinking and after some soul searching I decided to strike out on my own. Another interminable period and I came across a piece of an old rope/cork float and embraced it as a long lost relative.

Sense of direction of course was negative, so I had no idea whether I was miles from the original scene, or just yards. It didn't matter too much, I was alive, so there was hope.

After an extended relationship with my new-found friend, the piece of rope, I struck out again; don't know again how long for, but I looked up and there, some half mile away, was the outline of a destroyer HMS *Jervis*. Never in the whole of my naval career was I so glad to see one of His Majesty's ships. I don't know how long I was in the water, but it was dark when I went in and it was dark when I was dragged out. So it was not longer than all night, was it?

It was little consolation to find out some time later that the U-boat that sank us was later rammed and sunk, with no survivors, by one of our escorting destroyers, HMS *Sikh*. But a cruiser for a submarine was a pretty poor rate of exchange.

I was dragged aboard the *Jervis* like the proverbial drowned rat, taken below and a hot cup of tea put in my hand. As the hot liquid went down and hit my stomach, it made the return journey within a second. It was only then I realized I had swallowed a lot of fuel oil. My stomach was full of it. They hastened me to the sick bay. Now the *Jervis* had picked up a number of survivors, probably about eighty, and the sick bay staff consisted of a young surgeon lieutenant and one sick berth attendant. They earned their pay that night, if they never had before. Among the queue of patients I rated very low, so after my stomach was empty, I was given a tot of rum in one hand whilst being injected in the opposite arm. A combination of the two and I was out like a light. I came round, wrapped in a blanket, laying on top of some high lockers.

Now whilst en-route back to Egypt, someone had gone round and made a list of all the *Naiad* survivors, name, rank, number and any other relevant information to be handed in on arrival, along with the bodies. But yours truly, being out to the world and out of sight to boot, was omitted from the list. So I was not on the survivors list, nor as it turned out, on the casualty list. I didn't exist, on paper anyway.

So back in Egypt and probably for the first and only time I was glad to see it. I spent a week or so in the desert, as near as we could get to a recuperation period, then into Sidi Bishr again. By this time I had been abroad for about two-and-a-half years and hoped I might get home for some leave, having been a survivor twice. This did eventually happen. I went down to Fort Kabrit on the canal zone and managed a passage to South Africa via Aden and Port Sudan aboard HMS *Glengyle*. I disembarked at Durban and spent the next three weeks under canvas on Durban race course. After two-and-a-half years of war, most of it under continuous fire, Durban was Heaven, yes with a capital H. The hospitality shown to us by the people of South Africa is one of my endearing memories. I met a lot of people and life became enjoyable again, all at little expense to myself. This was important to me, because, remember I still did not exist on paper, and was existing on casual payments of about 15s. per week. It was not until my return to the UK in July, 1942, that this situation was rectified.

There was an on-going link with South Africa for me personally. Some of the people I met in Durban were resident in a town called Brakpan in the Transvaal and, as a result of this friendship, I received parcels, mainly food, but other luxury goods as well. Never have I expressed my gratitude for these parcels, just never got round to it at the time, and the years went by without me ever expressing my thanks. So if anyone ever reads these ramblings, please tell them in

Brakpan that I love 'em

After all these years it seems churlish of me not to have written to someone in South Africa and expressed my thanks myself, but better late than never. I think it was the Womens' Institute of that town that deserved the thanks.

The next stage of my journey home was aboard HMT *Empress of Russia*. Incidentally, she had been the *Empress of Prussia* before the war, but the 'P' was expediently dropped. Ports of call were Cape Town (a few more lovely days) Port Harcourt (Nigeria) and Freetown (Sierra Leone). My twenty-first birthday coincided with the two days in Freetown but I couldn't get ashore; I could not even get water to drink, never mind anything stronger. So to Liverpool, in that strange land known as England.

Having mentioned the Greeks and Yugoslavians, I would say a word here about the Poles. One of the destroyers in the Eastern Med at this time was HMS *Garland,* entirely Polish manned and a very valuable unit of the fleet. Also on the way home aboard the *Empress of Russia* we took on a crowd of Polish airmen in Cape Town, several hundred as I remember, who had been incarcerated in Russian concentration camps since the fall of Poland in 1939. The Russians had released them to us after Germany attacked them, and they had journeyed to South Africa via Iraq and Iran. We brought them home for retraining into the Free Polish Forces.

They were in pretty poor shape but eager to get into the fray. Bear in mind that they had not set eyes on a woman, any woman of any sort, shape or size or colour, for two-and-a-half years. The South Africans would not allow them ashore in Cape Town and they were eventually turned loose in Liverpool!

I have previously mentioned being 'lost' after the *Naiad* went down, not 'belonging' to anyone. Because the U-boat that sunk us was in turn sunk with all hands, the Germans did not know they had sunk us, and so our loss was not announced in the UK until about three months later, and for this reason we were not allowed to write home. When it was announced on the radio, a neighbour ran into my mother with the news; my father was also at sea at this time. She, not having heard from me, assumed the worst; eventually she wrote to the Admiralty and Portsmouth (my depot) seeking news. The replies she received were totally contradictory. One said, 'Your son is not a survivor,' the other, 'Your son is not a casualty'. See what I mean by not existing? A few weeks later I walked in through the door. I belonged again!

There was an amusing sequel to all this but it did not emerge until 1986. Upon my mother's decease, when we were turning out her possessions, we came across the letter from the Commodore, Portsmouth, saying that they did not know at that stage where I was but would communicate further when they found me. But, and this is the funny bit, they said, 'If you find him before we do, would you let us know?' Such were the vagaries of war.

There was an extended connection with *Naiad,* well not that one exactly, but her successor. In the 1970s, whilst I was working from London, the current *Naiad* came into the Port of London, alongside HMS *Belfast,* for a one week courtesy visit and, via a work colleague who was in the Sea Cadet Corps, I was invited to pay them a visit. The new one was a destroyer, not a cruiser but with progress she was larger than 'my' *Naiad*. I thoroughly enjoyed that visit. It brought back so many memories, but what struck me was the terrific improvement in the standard of living, air-conditioned living spaces, air-conditioned dining rooms (that one was totally beyond my comprehension), air-conditioned engineer's office, air-conditioned enclosed bridge. Air-conditioned this air-conditioned that, it was a different world. Mind you, I don't think they were any happier or any more efficient than we were. That can be argued, but it is my opinion. I consumed some of their rum and did not perceive any difference in that. Well, I don't remember any difference. The rum 'ration' had by this time disappeared. I don't know where it came from, but produced it was on this occasion. Thank you *Naiad*.

It was revealed to me on this visit that they had been trying to trace survivors from their predecessor and at that time had only discovered two, myself and an elderly gent from New Malden. I quite expect that some others would have perished later in the war, and others scattered to the four corners, but it was thought provoking.

But one more did emerge in the mid 1980s from Australia. As the result of an article in *Navy News*, published monthly in Portsmouth, I received a letter from Melbourne, Australia, from a Ron Hutton, who had been a Royal Marine on the cruiser *Naiad* in 1942 when we were sunk. We corresponded for a while and reminisced somewhat as can be imagined, but we seem to have lost touch again of late. He was not in a good state of health, so I wonder after all this time if he has joined the rest. I wonder if I am the only one left after forty-seven years?

I did get a bit of leave when I got home, but already there was another ship awaiting my services so I did not get the survivor's leave due to me. I pursued the matter after the war and again in 1947 when in depot, but from that day to this I never did get that survivor's leave. In sailors' terminology 'I was seen orf!'

ABOUT THE ATLANTIC 1942-1943

That leave was all too short, certainly not long enough to properly recuperate. I was in a fairly poor state, mentally and physically whole, but the experiences of the past couple of years had left their mark internally. There was no immediate cure in sight either, for my next draft was to HMS *Gorleston Y92* and the next twelve months were spent on Atlantic convoys. A lot has been written about convoy work in the Atlantic, and a lot of films made, but in none of them was the stress factor overplayed. Our losses were horrific. Although personally I did not lose another ship, the experience did nothing to help my mental state, and it was not until about 1945 that I began to overcome the internal scars. I would just add here that at least I did make it to 1945, and give thanks.

The *Gorleston* turned out to be another of those anomalies that occur in war time. It will be remembered that Churchill did a deal with America; fifty of their old obsolete destroyers in exchange for bases in the West Indies, the Bahamas mainly. We were so desperately short of ships for escort duties that probably it was a good deal, although subsequently it was revealed that those destroyers did not, shall we say, 'come up to spec'.

What was not so widely known is that part of the deal included ten old US Coastguard cutters. We renamed them after coastguard stations around the UK. Totland, Hartland,

Walney, etc and of course Gorleston. They were built for inshore coastal work and never intended for the abuse they received from us Brits. They were only about eight hundred ton and with a low draft and high freeboard. Consequently, it was said, they would roll on damp grass. So life was pretty unpleasant for the crews in wild Atlantic weather. Propulsion was turbo-electric. New to us and lessons had to be learned – quickly.

I went over to Londonderry, which of course was the escort base for Atlantic convoys, to find, as had happened before, that she was out, and not expected back for two or three weeks. So I was billeted there to await her return. I got in a bit of football there, including a trial match for Derry City in the Irish League. As a result of that game I was invited to keep in touch on future visits to Derry with a view to guest appearances, prevalent in all league clubs during the war. But I was never able to take up the offer; circumstances just did not allow. Pity, I would have enjoyed that.

About Londonderry. We always returned there after each 'job' and, except for a couple of occasions when we went to Immingham to dock, and once when we were in Liverpool, Derry was as near home as we ever got. We were so glad to see it, steaming up the Foyle after a convoy. We always had a welcome; we would arrive with sometimes six weeks' pay in our pockets. About £5. Wow! The last of the big spenders!

A few of us had a favourite pub, Ma Martins. Do you know after 1943 I never went to Derry again until 1960. I looked up Ma's place then and she still remembered me. Yes, I have a soft spot for Derry and its people; what a tragedy the current situation is.

During these twelve months we took convoys to Iceland, Russia (phew), West Africa and the West Indies. We also caught the invasion of Algiers. The first two were straight there and straight back, geographically that is, but with the others the route was a bit more devious as to get south you had to go north first.

We would pick up the convoys on either the Mersey or Clyde, then proceed northwards; Iceland, Greenland, Canada, US then from the Caribbean, if proceeding further, a mad dash across mid-Atlantic. All this was designed to confuse and dodge the U-boat packs. If possible we would seek out bad weather, as they then found it difficult to operate. We would be hounded incessantly on leaving European waters, but even more so on return by the same circuitous route.

Occasionally we would get a glimpse of the world untroubled by war – the US or Canada – and how wonderful it was to find towns with street lights on. But it was usually a brief stop for fuel, and if we got ashore it was just for a couple of hours.

There was one exception, one occasion, when we did get a few days' break. The West Indies convoys were of course all tankers. We would arrive in the North Caribbean and steam southwards, dropping off a couple of empty tankers at islands such as Trinidad and Jamaica, the last stop off being Aruba and Curacao. The latter was invariably our destination. The break was only a few days, but it was wonderful. The Dutch were very hospitable, and one left there refreshed a little and fortified for the journey home, ready to face yet another hammering.

With war time security, our destination would never be revealed until we were actually en route, but there was inevitable conjecture as we met the convoy at either Mersey or Clyde. If they were all tankers, well West Indies here we come.

Conjecture was rife when we picked up an unusually large convoy off Greenock, which consisted mainly of large liners converted to troopships, and bristling with soldiers and all their equipment and smaller vehicles. Ah, this is something big, we thought, something out of the ordinary. Still we had no idea where we were heading. We followed the usual route north, down the east coast of America, the usual dash across the Atlantic, still no ideas. I wondered if the troops in the convoy knew what was to be their destiny. Gibraltar? There was some swopping round of personnel there in the Straits and we in fact embarked a number of soldiers. Then we headed east, still no idea. A lot of suggestions were made, Italy, Southern France, all wrong. We were embarked upon the invasion of Algiers.

Whilst the main invasion took place along the beaches adjacent to Algiers, three of the cutters went straight into the harbour and landed our troops there, right in the heart. One cutter was sunk, but we got out unscathed. We also had the satisfaction of shooting down one of the German planes that was attacking us, rescued the pilot, and handed him over to the army.

No sooner were we out of Algiers when it was back to the UK with a few hours stop-over for fuel in Gibraltar. During that few hours I had a visitor on board, my father. We had about an hour's conversation. He was stationed at Europa Point signal station at the time and managed to get a boat out to *Gorleston*. One hour, and that was the only time we met during the entire war. We were not to meet again until 1946.

So, it was back to the Clyde and another convoy straight back to Algiers, this time with reinforcements for the 1st Army, the landing having been consolidated. This time on the way home we passed the lights of Gibraltar at night on Christmas Day. Nostalgic, but that was as near to Christmas as we were to get. However, we did arrive in Londonderry on New Year's Eve. Good old Derry, and we were even more glad to see it than usual. I think we all had a memorable New Year's Eve – I don't remember a thing.

I did yet another trip back to Algiers with more men and equipment, but by this time the 1st Army had advanced well along the coast and we were more in control of the situation on land and sea. This trip passed without incident.

One small point on the Algiers landings that I would comment on. Over the intervening years I have read statement and counter-statement over the fact that some British troops were sent ashore in American uniforms. The supposition was that they would receive more welcome from the French citizens, the memories of Casablanca and Mers-el-Kibir still being fresh. I believe this was officially denied but it *was* so. I know what I saw.

To summarize the Battle of the Atlantic from our point of view. I had a year of it. I went into it on not too good a mental state and for me it was a constant personal battle, living on a knife edge, life and death continuously so close to one another. Not that I was much different from most others involved, I hasten to add, and thankful to have survived it.

It was on one of these latter visits to Algiers that I first met Marcel Cerdan, then a French matelot, later to become world middle-weight champion. We met again briefly in 1949 in Marseille. He is now probably not so well known as a boxer as for his long running affair with singer Edith Piaf. Funny what one is remembered for, isn't it? There was a man who achieved so much, but is remembered for something totally opposed to his achievements. Guess the popular press has to answer for that one.

I left *Gorleston* late 1943 and took a long journey – Derry to Larne by train, ferry to Stranraer, train to Portsmouth and Carlisle, Liverpool, Birmingham, Bath, Bristol and Winchester, back to Pompey. That was quite typical of war time journeys; it took twenty-four hours and ordinary trains would be, without warning, shunted into a siding for long periods whilst the vital weapons or materials hogged the main lines. Rightly so, of course, but you never knew; you just sat there waiting for movement.

I had a bit of a break from war now, a three month promotion course in Portsmouth. I even managed a few weekends at home, but like most courses in wartime it was condensed. Naval manpower was at a premium so you were sent back to sea with all haste. But it was good to be on *terra firma*.

1943-1946: THE EASTERN MED. AGAIN

HMS *Blenheim,* she was an ex-MN ship, the SS *Achilles,* Blue Funnel Line, the navy had converted her into a sort of general purpose ship; well that's the best description I can think of, a bit of everything. I joined her in Govan Dock, Glasgow, and had a few weeks there before sailing. Glasgow is another city I have a bit of a soft spot for. I was to spend a lot more time there after the war, but on this occasion it was a welcome breather before re-entering the fray.

We left the Clyde once again with no knowledge of our destination. The Far East was the most prevalent 'buzz' but like most buzzes it was way off line.

First stop was Gibraltar. *Blenheim* was a coal-fired vessel; in fact her boilers were the largest, in capacity and sheer size, that the navy ever had. So Gibraltar was a coaling stop. If one has never experienced coaling a large vessel, it is difficult to imagine such an operation; certainly it is extremely difficult to explain it with the written word. You live, breathe and eat coal dust, not only during the operation, but for days afterwards. It is in your eyes, ears and every other aperture that nature created. Clothing becomes impregnated with it, every mouthful of food has coal dust in it. But as day succeeds day, the ever present menace gradually subsides. Then, after a few days perhaps, even weeks, it is time to coal ship again.

I had experienced it in the hoppers previously so I was not unused to it, but it is never a pleasant experience. Remember that this was for twenty-four hours a day; no coming off shift after eight hours for a break, bath, food and whatever. You lived with it, no choice.

Next stop Malta, then Alexandria. It was here that any conjecture as to our destination was dispelled. It was to be the Eastern Med. fleet again. Mind you, the Eastern Med. fleet of 1943-1944 was a totally different proposition to my previous spell there. The army was by now in control of the entire North African coast and our journey eastwards was uneventful. I couldn't believe my eyes. No Stukas? Well just the odd few maybe, but what a difference that eighteen months had made.

So this was to be my domain until the end of the war. There was action but this time on the European side of the Med. Italy and Yugoslavia come to mind and a landing near Dubrovnik, but now it was more on our terms. There was resistance, of course there was, but we now held the aces and it made all the difference.

I had spells on other ships, as before in this war zone. The destroyer *Eridge* was one and a second spell on the *Carlisle*. But in general this commission was far more low key than my previous one. There was the ever present thought that we may move on to the Far East theatre of operation, but it never came, and I was not to see the Far East for several more years. I did not have any grave misgivings over that.

Whilst on the subject of *Blenheim,* there is a story worth telling; a ghost story, a true ghost story. When we, the navy took it over (the ship, not the ghost) from the Blue Funnel Line we also took over the legend of the Chinese fireman apparition; remember that being on the UK/China run, she had a Chinese crew.

A slight knowledge of the ship's layout is advisable to understand the story. There was this very large boiler room, containing the three double ended boilers, three furnaces each end of each boiler, eighteen furnaces in total. The engine room, situated aft, was separated from the boiler room by a series of ready-use coal bunkers, the whole complex being surrounded, port and starboard, by storage bunkers. Communication between boiler and engine room was by a tunnel running through the ready-use bunkers.

The legend stated that on a certain night in the late 1930s, whilst the ship was en route eastwards through the Arabian Sea, two Chinese firemen, between whom existed bad blood due to some loss of face, got to blows whilst on watch in the boiler room. One attacked the other with his shovel, and killed him, and to cover his crime, secreted the body deep into one of the ready-use bunkers. We never did find out whether the body was ever discovered and if so what was the eventual outcome.

The authenticity of the story is beyond doubt, but that was where the story finished. No one knew of the ultimate conclusion. One wonders if the culprit was dealt with by relatives of the victim on arrival in China, whether he jumped over the side in anticipation of such reprisals or, perish the thought, maybe he is still alive, wandering around somewhere. I merely pass on the legend as it was passed to us.

Back to the story. One night whilst in Alexandria in middle watch (0000-0400) we were auxiliary steaming, I was in charge and things were fairly quiet. Then one of the stokers asked me if the ghost story was true. 'Of course,' I said.

'Have you ever seen it?' they asked.

'Yes, last year,' was my reply. 'About this time.'

Next question was, 'What was it like, what did it do?'. Trying hard to be complacent about the whole thing, I told them that on the anniversary of the murder, said ghost emerged from said bunker with a ghostly shovel in his hand, went right round the boiler room and fired all eighteen furnaces and it was about this time of year.

I must have been convincing because an incredulous silence fell over my audience. They sat there, mouths agape. 'Why should you worry?' I told them, 'Every shovelful that he fires is one less shovelful for you to shift. You should be

The author, then an Engine room Petty Officer, 1944

grateful to him.'

Well, a computer could not have timed it better. Several tons of coal, built up at the side of the bunker, suddenly shifted and rumbled down to the bunker floor. Of course on a ship, the effect of this (and it happened not infrequently) was for the ship to give a fairly violent shudder, and the effect on my watch was likewise. Pausing very briefly for a glance up at the bunker in anticipation of our ethereal friend, they dashed for the tunnel into the engine room. But none of them overtook me.

As the intensity of battle decreased in this area of operations, there became more time for leisure activities and swimming featured strongly, as the facilities were to hand. Many off duty periods have I spent at Stanley Bay, a few miles out of Alexandria and several other beaches in that area. Sporting competition came more to the fore. With so many service men still in the Middle East competition became fierce and the general standard was high in all sports. Soccer for example; an all services soccer team was formed mainly for exhibition matches against, for example, the Egyptian side. It was called The Wanderers, and contained nearly all top class pre-war professionals. Names that come to mind include Tom Finney, Andy McLaren, Wille Redpath and George Male on one occasion. They don't come any better than that, and when they played they drew very large gates.

At *Blenheim* level, we were in the Middle East Forces League and on the last season finished runners-up. We were also runners-up in the knock-out cup. Not a bad season's achievement by anybody's standards. I played all over the area, including some unlikely pitches up in the desert against army sides.

I enjoyed my football, but in retrospect, the war stunted my progress in the sport. This applies to most of my generation I guess. When war broke out I was eighteen; when it finished I was nearly twenty-four. In any hard contact sport, those are your best years gone down the drain. But as I have said before, and will never lose sight of, I am here, many are not.

The same concepts applied to my boxing career, such as it was. At eighteen I had a certain amount of promise, but at twenty-four, after a physical and mental hammering for years, I was out of it. I managed to continue in both sports for a number of years afterwards but any pretension to greatness, if it existed in the first place, was gone. The last time I pulled the gloves on, albeit in an exhibition, I was about thirty-nine, so I figure I didn't do too badly – considering.

Back to the late wartime. There came to join *Blenheim*, a young cockney stoker by the name of Edward Govier. How he came to join us is a long and not over-happy story, but he had been boxing professionally in the Merseyside area immediately prior to joining us and was unbeaten in nine pro fights, meeting and beating some of the top pro flyweights. One who comes to mind was Joe Curran, a name well respected in the sport. Incidentally, the promoter in Merseyside was my old acquaintance of 1939, Johnny Best, no less.

On arrival in Egypt the lad immediately enquired as to where he could get good training facilities and future contests. He was sent to me as someone having contacts. Now one of these contacts was a guy who owned a bar in the dock area of Alexandria by the name of George Aziz. Boxing fans will know that name, not as a bar owner, but as a very good bantam-featherweight who campaigned in England in the mid 30s with fair success, meeting such names as Johnny King and Nel Tarleton, names legendary in boxing. I saw him once in this period at Blackfriars Ring.

Govier's professional name was Terry Allen. In the immediate post-war years his career progressed at some pace and he eventually became world champion. I like to think, rightly or wrongly, that I played a small part in all this. He lost his title but got a second bash at it, this time in Tokyo. Yoshio Shirai was the holder by then. I was in Japan at the time, but many miles from Tokyo, and tried desperately to see the fight. I could have got there, but as *Comus* was sailing next morning, I would not get back in time. Never mind!

But I digress; back to Egypt. George Aziz and I took Terry, as I will refer to him henceforth, to a local gym for a perusal. We were impressed. Were we impressed! George then undertook to arrange future contests in Egypt; he played it very cool locally and matched Terry with care, bearing in mind that he was unknown in the Middle East. I know George made a bit of money backing Terry locally until his fame spread a bit. The result of this for yours truly was a lot of free drinks. For the rest of my spell there, if I cared to use George's bar which rejoiced in the name of The Black Cat, I was always received with due reverence. Nuff said!

Another boxing character I met in this period was Ali Khalil, a top amateur heavyweight in this part of the world, who ran an open air gymnasium in Alexandria. We got on well and Terry trained there quite a bit. He never took a penny from me in gym fees, not at all the general practice.

Mustapha Ezzat was another. I believe he had boxed for Egypt in the 1936 Olympic Games in Berlin and when Terry became known and his local invincibility was established, the press cry was for Ezzat to emerge from retirement and put this Englishman in his place. He was by this time an officer of the Egyptian Army. The contest eventually took place in Cairo; only one winner though and it was not Ezzat.

To illustrate the superiority Terry had over any opposition that could be found for him, it was revealed on arrival at his first contest under the auspices of George Aziz that his opponent was a featherweight at nine stone, exactly one stone over our boy's weight, and that is a lot amongst the little men. George shrugged off our objections. Don't worry, he said, and smiled.

When we got into the ring, despite assurances that everything was 'laid on' for us, all that was in the corner was a bucket of water, no bottle, no sponge, nothing. So as the bell went to commence the contest I said to the other second, 'I'll nip back to the dressing room and see what I can lay my hands on.' I did just that, down the tunnel, into the dressing room. I grabbed a sponge and an empty lemonade bottle, back up the tunnel and just as I emerged into the stadium, a roar shook the place and before me was said local featherweight flat on his back, out to the world. It had taken just one punch.

There was I, the chief second, and I had not seen a blow struck.

Incidentally, the promoter at the Municipal Stadium was on a good thing. He matched the local boys against British and other service men. One side of the stadium would be packed with service men who came to see the locals thrashed, the other side packed with locals who came to see us thrashed. The turnstiles clicked away merrily. He couldn't lose.

Our 'purse' for these fights was £2. But as the locals were all amateur, they got a cup or medal. To get round the rules we were also presented with a cup, which was taken from you in the dressing room and exchanged for £2. The cup was then transferred to ringside, in a sack, ready for the next contestant. Duplicity? Guess it goes on all over the world.

So time came to end the hostilities. V/E day came and went, likewise V/J day. The joy expressed on these occasions by the forces was something to remember. I have seen pictures of the scenes in London at the time, but they no way surpassed the jubilation in Alexandria. There was a lot of 'sorting out' to be done around the world, but now there was hope. One could put the pain and suffering into the background and start to make plans with a reasonable assumption as to their fruition.

During this period I won myself a place in the Engineering School, based in Devonport, for a two year course, and was looking forward to returning to the UK to take up the position. I was eventually relieved and returned home, taking passage from Port Said, via Gibraltar to Portsmouth, on HMS *Slinger*. She was an escort aircraft carrier, in fact an old Liberty ship with a flight deck stuck on the top, and internal adaptations. Another war-dictated anomaly. She was a great ship. She brought me home, didn't she?

It was early 1946, but before proceeding with the next chapter, there is one more story I must tell. It involves the last bit of the journey home, the train from Portsmouth to London. I alighted at Surbiton, there to catch a bus to West Ewell, where my parents now resided. A very few miles, the last 'little' bit of the journey home. I boarded the bus, well loaded after so long away, two-and-a-half years, to find my suitcase would not go into the luggage space under the stairs; there was already too much luggage there. So I put it down immediately outside the platform. I went upstairs, as there were no seat available downstairs. I had not been seated for many minutes when the conductor came up and bawled as loud as he could, 'Whose is that green case down there?' There was only one obvious owner – me, and he fixed me with a withering stare.

The entire load of passengers looked at me, waiting for a response. My conductor 'friend' continued, 'If it ain't removed straight away, I will chuck it off into the road.' Red blood welled up into my brain, I could not believe my ears, that I was being treated this way.

Go ahead,' I said, 'chuck it off, but you will go off after it,' and drew myself up to my full height, 5'5". The other passengers were behind me unanimously. 'Go on sailor, you don't deserve that treatment,' they said. My case was still there when I alighted. I had won the moral battle.

But such was the hero's return to his native land.

2

Aftermath and Peaceful Pursuit
1946-1952

After some leave it was off to the West Country for the next two years to study engineering. I did not find it easy. It was a highly concentrated course, five-and-a-half days a week, three evenings a week and in addition the schedule required at least two hours swotting every evening. Some of my contemporaries seemed to have photographic memories, it all came so easy to them, but I was not that fortunate. I had to really hammer it into my brain, but I consoled myself with the fact that the knowledge, having been hammered in, did not have much chance of escape.

Ultimately I got good marks, which is what matters. In fact I was never out of the top three in engineering theory or practice, but I am afraid maths dragged me down to about fifth place overall.

Whilst on this course, we lived virtually as civilians. I had to find digs which was not too difficult and I was quite lucky there. I had three different digs and had no complaint about any of them. Wartime rationing and restrictions were still on, but after the previous six years life was returning to normal. For myself, I really enjoyed this period.

I got in quite a bit of football in this period in the local league. We did reasonably well and it was enjoyable. I still remember one match in Torquay, when with the score 1-1 and only minutes to go, an opposing forward broke clear and was about to score. Yours truly was in no position to stop him. I was several feet behind in the pursuit but as he raised his foot for the shot, I literally threw myself at him. I gave away a free kick, but I had stopped a certain score. As I got up from the ground I suddenly realized that the other chap was still there, stiff.

At the moment of impact, his body had 'given' but his head tended to stay where it was, if you see what I mean. He was removed on a stretcher but very thankfully we were told before we left that he was OK. As the stretcher was being carried away, his wife dashed on to the field to attack me. It did end up amicably, thank goodness. Funny the things you remember, isn't it?

Another big event occurred in my life at this time. I got 'spliced'. I am still in that happy state and have two daughters and five grandchildren to perpetuate the line. Things were not easy in the early stages; housing was very short, and we started married life in a tiny flat in Devonport, but at least we could see light at the end of the tunnel, after so long without much to look forward to.

At the end of the two years, I did another short course at a RN establishment at Corsham, Wilts. One of the instructors was a certain young Lieutenant Mountbatten who was courting a certain young lady by the name of Princess Elizabeth. In fact their engagement was announced on the day I left.

I was due a long spell at sea after qualifying, and certainly got it. My first draft was to the old and venerable battleship HMS *Nelson*. It was a fairly uneventful spell which culminated in her steaming up to Inverkeithing, north of the Forth Bridge, to be scrapped. A sad nostalgic task this to see such a grand old ship end her days that way. It was rather like taking an old and trusty steed to the knacker's yard to be turned into tins of pet food.

Back to Pompey to join aircraft carrier HMS *Illustrious*. I changed over half way through the commission to HMS *Implacable*. The *Implacable* had been refitting in Devonport and on completion was to become Home Fleet flagship, the first time a carrier had carried out this function but this was inevitable with the demise of the big capital ships, the battle wagons. But there was a snag; by tradition the flagship had to be a Portsmouth ship, as the senior depot, so the two ships had to change crews. The big change-over took place alongside in Rosyth. Quite an operation to complete in a day,

The author, on the right, as a member of the Home Fleet Boxing Team, 1949-50.

twelve hundred men and all their belongings and equipment.

The period on *Illustrious* was an active one, plenty of sport, particularly on calls into Invergordon on the Moray Firth. The Admiralty sports facilities there were excellent and I played a lot of football, and was involved in boxing (when was I not?), training youngsters by this time. The facilities on a big ship are far greater than a destroyer; to have part of an aircraft hanger available as a gym was an unknown luxury up till now.

The prime function of an aircraft carrier is of course to provide a platform for the Fleet Air Arm. I learned to 'take my hat off' to those pilots. That carrier deck must look awfully small from up there and it might be rolling and pitching at the same time. In anything like bad weather it must be horrendous to look down and try to land a plane on it. But as to the rest of the Fleet Air Arm, they were considered a bit of a pampered class by the rest of us.

We got around UK waters a fair bit; ports of call included Portsmouth, Plymouth, Portland, Dartmouth, Invergordon, Fishguard, Caernarvon Bay, Bigbury Bay and Rosyth.

So to the *Implacable,* more interesting for me anyway. By this time I was Home Fleet boxing trainer and had some really useful lads. We competed in the UK widely and a few times in the Med. with a fair amount of success. I would emphasize that all this was in spare time, all strictly amateur. We still had a ship to sail from A to B.

It was also made more interesting by the greater divergence of horizon. During this spell we caught two of the annual Home Fleet/Med. Fleet exercises, in which one fleet attacked the Straits of Gibraltar whilst the other defended. There was great rivalry between the two forces and the competition at sea was surpassed only by the competition ashore in Gibraltar after the 'battle'. The two fleets met at practically all sports and at varying levels, the whole culminating in the boxing match which took place in the old coal sheds on the quayside. It was cut-throat. There was more at stake than the trophies. Pride. No way would you submit to 'them' as long as there was breath in your body.

Although we were Home Fleet, a look at the ports of call in the Med. will show that we really did get around. As well as Gibraltar and Malta, there was Tangiers, Oran, Mers-el-Kibir, Malaga, Villefranche-sur-mer, Nice, Monte Carlo, Sardinia, Marseilles. Variety is the spice of life.

There are a few interesting tales emerging from these visits. One was during a visit to Tangiers, then a freeport where 'anything goes' was the watchword. Four of us embarked on a bar crawl of the Old Medina. We embarked on a campaign of sampling new drinks. Old as the hills no doubt, but new to us. We quickly found out the the Spanish for four was quatro, so we would point to the bottle containing a drink we had not tried, and say to the barman, 'Quatro.' It worked well. We sampled a lot of new drinks, some good, some terrible, but most intermediate and not terribly memorable.

Later on in the day we were joined by five shipmates in the bar of the moment. We had just discovered another new drink and they looked at it and said, 'That looks interesting, what is it?' The fellow whose round it was went up to the bar to

HMS *Implacable* at anchor in Villefranche, 1950

purchase nine of this new-found concoction. I went with him and wondered how he was going to convey that we wanted nine. He pointed to the bottle and said, 'Quatro twice plus one.' Would you believe it, we got nine! Resourcefulness? Well, had you been that barman you would have counted the heads and served accordingly, wouldn't you?

Whilst recounting humorous experiences, I had another in Nice. We were anchored off Villefranche and used to go into Nice or Monte Carlo for some evenings, but had to catch the last bus back, which from Nice was 2300, or be stuck for the night. This particular evening we came out of a nice quiet bar in a side street to get back to the bus station, but within minutes realized that we had lost all sense of direction and did not know which way to head. Time was getting very short and we looked for someone to ask. Not a soul in sight, never is on those occasions. However, to our rescue came a young lady, round a corner in our direction. 'You ask her,' said my companions, 'you know enough French.'

So, as she came towards us I mentally rehearsed what I was going to say. I must have got it right because she looked at me for a few seconds and said, 'Yes, that was very good, but do you mind if I answer you in English. I happen to come from Brighton.'

Currency in foreign ports was quite a problem at this time. We were only allowed to change an amount equivalent to the amount of time we were to spend in a port of call; i.e. one week in France – one week's pay in francs. This was due to currency restrictions in force at the time. This often restricted our purchasing power. In Tangiers things were very cheap; this was the headquarters of the western world smuggling industry and you could buy Swiss watches, for example, at less than half the price they would cost in Switzerland. But in France we were in the pauper class. The French, like us, were struggling to recover from the war.

I have another fond memory, this one Mers-el-Kibir. I got involved with the French Foreign Legion and went to Sidi-bel-Abbes, the Legion headquarters in North Africa. I came away as a Member of Honour and there are not too many of those around. No big heroics were involved, I hasten to add. But one to add to life's store of experiences. I still have photographs of us on the parade ground at Sidi-bel-Abbes with some Legionnaires.

Whilst on the subject of the Legion, a fairly large proportion of them at this time were German. Most of them had extricated themselves from Allied hands at the end of the war and escaped retribution in the anonymity of the Foreign Legion.

☆ ☆ ☆

There came a new Commander-in-Chief to the Home Fleet about this time – Admiral Sir Rhoderick Macgrigor, affectionately known as 'Wee Mac' due to his diminutive stature. He soon made it clear we would be spending more time in Scotland now, and so it was. The Forth area – Rosyth; the Clyde area – Glasgow, Greenock and Gourock, Invergordon, Lossiemouth, Oban, Aberdeen and Buckie. Add to that lot Weymouth, Plymouth, Dartmouth, Bangor (N.I.), Penzance and of course Portsmouth, to say nothing of Oslo and Bergen in Norway. We really showed the flag a bit.

I liked Norway and met a lot of people there. At the time, they were a little impoverished after the war, but I have been back there since on several occasions and they seem prosperous enough now. The Norwegians I have met – business and pleasure – have always been welcoming and their scenery . . . I don't know of any better.

It was at this time, or thereabouts, that NATO was formed and the first big NATO naval exercise took place in June 1949. It was mounted from Mounts Bay, Cornwall, with over a hundred ships taking part from all countries then in the alliance. *Implacable* was flag ship for the exercise, so accordingly we carried a number of top military observers, as well as a fairly large military press contingent. At the head of the observers was Lord Montgomery, who at the time was deputy C in C NATO, Eisenhower being the 'boss'. Prince Bernhardt of the Netherlands was another observer I remember.

I had a visit from 'Monty' one afternoon during the exercise. He had apparently expressed a wish on the bridge to visit the engine room. This was typical of the man, in my opinion; bored with all the bull on the upper deck, he wanted to see what made things work. 'The Guts', as he called it.

The bridge phoned me asking if he could come down. I replied in the affirmative of course, but asked that it be made clear to him that there would be no protocol observed down here; no one would spring to attention for him; we were too busy. They said he was aware of this. The carrier was 'flying' at the time, and when planes are taking off or landing a red light shows in the engine room, and it is no exaggeration to say that a pilot's life can depend upon 'digits being extracted' during this operation by the engine room staff. I warned my lads of the impending visit, telling them that if spoken to they were only to give him their attention if consistent with their duties.

He duly arrived and stood unobtrusively in the background for some time, probably about an hour, taking it all in. Very correctly he only spoke to my staff when he saw that they were not otherwise occupied. Personally I took no part in it at all, taking the view that if he wanted my attention he would approach me. I was fully occupied anyway.

When he had seen enough, he turned to go back up the gangway, stopped after two rungs, looked over at me, retraced his steps, walked over to me and stood about a foot away. No word was spoken. He looked me up and down. I thought to myself, I am going to get told off any minute for ignoring him totally. But no! He looked me straight in the eyes and said, 'Well done!' Then disappeared up the ladder.

There is a day, a Sunday if my memory serves me well, that is in the annals of post-war naval history I feel sure. It is well embedded in my naval history anyway. HMS *Illustrious*, with most of the rest of the Home Fleet, lay quietly at anchor in Portland Harbour. There was a bit of a blow coming across the Chesil Beach, across the Bank and between Weymouth and Portland (nothing much, about force four or five). Liberty men were landed as usual during the day at Weymouth Pier. We had been at anchor for several days, and this particular day was the only one I did not go ashore. More evidence, if it were needed, that someone up there kept a kindly eye on me. For disaster was about to strike.

The first boat to return liberty men, about 2100, crossed the harbour without problems, as the wind, which was increasing in force by the hour, was astern, and once out of the harbour and into the bay they were protected. But the return journey was a different proposition altogether. The wind by now was force eight or nine. Across the bay was easy, but as the cutter turned into Portland Harbour through the breakwater, she hit the gale bows on. They did not stand a chance and were quickly engulfed by the heavy seas. She went down rapidly. A few survived but twenty-nine were drowned.

There were some heroics enacted that night. One Royal Marine dived off the *Illustrious* and carried out some rescues. Three times, I think, he went over and rescued many. I wish I could remember his name.

The inevitable inquiry took place and the coxswain of the boat, a poor little midshipman, carried the can. He drowned, so he could not give evidence on his own behalf. We all thought he had been harshly dealt with posthumously. A scapegoat had to be found and he was it.

This tragic accident did bring home to me the fact that the press sometimes get it all wrong. We read of happenings in the papers, daily, and accept them as true. But press reports of the

Illustrious incident, all of them, were woefully short of the truth.

Personally I could quote many press reports as inaccurate, but most were in wartime, and the necessity for some was accepted. There were times when it was necessary or expedient to put out false reports of happenings, sometimes to lay a false scent to the enemy, and occasionally to allay fears in the civilian population at home. But on this occasion, we could not see that it was necessary or expedient. All was revealed to the inquiry anyway. It was difficult to understand why the reporting was so far from the truth.

And so in late 1950 I left *Implacable*, and returned inevitably to Portsmouth, back to base. That was the end of my 'big' ship era. *Nelson, Illustrious* and *Implacable*. Good experience, useful experience, but for me, well, it was rather like an extension of barrack life. Too big, too much 'bull'. I much preferred life on a smaller ship, about destroyer size. Life was a lot harder on small ships, but the comradeship made up for a lot. A man could be 'lost' on a large ship for two years and not know half of his shipmates. In later years I have met people who in course of conversation have revealed that they served on HMS so and so in 1950, and we would find that we had been shipmates for a year and never set eyes on one another. This would not be possible on a destroyer. Of course, in today's navy they only have about one capital ship in commission at a time, so I guess it does not arise. Not so much anyway.

An old, and oft used quotation states that after the Lord Mayor's Show comes the muck cart, and so it was in my career. After the big ships my next appointment was to the other end of the social scale – tank landing craft. There were twenty-eight of them; landing ships and landing craft at anchor in the Gareloch, Scotland, and that was my next job. They lay just as they finished the war. It was uncanny to walk aboard and find things in living spaces just as they had been left; pin-ups on the bulkheads, long forgotten girlfriends' photos inside locker doors and even half eaten meals on tables. Such had been the hurry to get crews demobbed once hostilities had ceased in 1945.

There were a lot of other ships in reserve at this time in the Gareloch, the battleship *King George V* amongst them. Some would be re-commissioned shortly as the inevitability of the

Korean War loomed large, some were shortly destined for the scrapyard.

As for the tank landing vessels, it was decided at high level that they could well be needed again shortly in Korea, and a programme was launched to refit them totally, bring them up to modern requirements, then put them back into reserve. This time they were to be ready for use as required, just put a crew aboard, supplies and ammunition, and they would be ready for the off. This work was to be carried out in various civilian shipyards up and down the Clyde and this is where I came in. My job was to oversee these refits as Admiralty representative. It was a good job. I lived at the York Hotel in Glasgow as each vessel was refitted, returning to Gareloch on completion until the next one came 'up the river', to use a good old Glasgow expression.

I enjoyed my time in Glasgow. As already stated I have a soft spot for the place. The city was at the height of its 'bad name' era at this time and I saw some horrible things. I saw a man razored for no apparent reason one night, a slash to the bone on one cheek. On another occasion I inadvertently walked into a full scale gang fight, where axes and bicycle chains were the main weapons, as well as bottles. The 'Polis' were in evidence and had the battleground surrounded and sealed off, waiting for the blood letting to subside before moving in to make arrests. I didn't blame them for that. I just stood transfixed as the warfare ebbed and flowed almost in front of me.

But the average Glaswegian was not of this ilk. Most that I met were easy to get along with, at work and play, and I met a lot of them. I managed to get home about once a month or so during this period. It was a welcome break before my involvement in the Korean war.

One of the LCTs (landing craft tanks) was kept in commission for the training of army commandos. We would leave the Gareloch, pick up the troops in Greenock, hare across the Clyde estuary to the Isle of Arran and land them at Brodick Bay, Lamlash or Holy Isle. They would then charge up the mountain and 'capture' their objective. It was an ideal training ground for the army, in mostly ideal but variable conditions.

The sporting scene was a bit quiet for me. I did not

participate much but I don't think I missed a Scottish Home International at Hampden Park during this period. I enjoyed them all – the Scottish Cup Final, Scottish League Cup Final, I saw them all.

Boxing also: the big name in Scottish boxing at this time was Peter Keenan and I saw him win the British title, defend it in his next fight and win the European title in his next against Luis Romero. Some years later I met Luis Romero again in Barcelona. He had an establishment just off the Plaza de Cataluna in that city.

There was one small incident on the sporting scene that for me was memorable. Also resident at the York Hotel was a track athlete, an Englishman who, at that time was Scottish champion, due to residence qualifications. He coaxed me into doing some road work with him, just to keep him in trim during the winter. It just so happened that there was a big boxing promotion coming up at the Kelvin Hall featuring Danny Womber, an American in the Sugar Ray Robinson school, against a West Ham battler called Bob Frost.

Well, as we plodded round the streets, yours truly in navy jersey with a towel wrapped round his neck must have looked the typical pugilist in training and, before I realized it, I was trailed by a load of Glasgow kids asking for my autograph. They had heard me in conversation with my colleague and jumped to the conclusion that I was Bob Frost. Sorry Bob!

The west of Scotland is a beautiful part of the world and I was fortunate enough to see a fair bit of it during this spell. Whilst in the Gareloch, during autumn and winter, we would look up at the hills each morning and study the current snow line to assess how long we had before it got down to our bank. Then surely one crisp morning there it was. From then onwards, of course, life became a little more tedious, but nevertheless it was very beautiful.

It was during this time I concluded my contract with Her Majesty's Navy after twelve years. I joined up in 1939. I suppose I would have signed on for the next ten years but fate took a hand here and made the decision for me. The Korean war had started and no regular servicemen were allowed discharge at all. This pushed me over the brink. I reasoned that if I was to serve another two or three years, or whatever, I might as well sign on and get a pension out of it.

Having got me committed, the navy did not lose much time in getting me to Korea and there lies the next chapter of this story.

But before moving on, I referred to *Her* Majesty's Navy. This was so, *just.* I remember it so well. Whilst walking up from Queen's Dock in Glasgow, back to my hotel, I passed an old lady on a street corner, sobbing her heart out. 'What's the trouble love?' I said, expecting to be told of some family tragedy.

'Just heard it on the radio,' she said, 'the King is dead. That poor girl will have to take over now.'

I was quite moved by that lovely old lady's concern.

3

The Far East
1952-1955

HMS *Comus* (pennant no D20) destroyer of the CO/CH class, 1,800 tons, I think. A good class of destroyer, and in general a good ship to serve on; not too big to attract too much 'bull', not too small that living was too hard. Altogether not bad.

It depended of course on the ship's company; a good skipper can make a ship; a bad one, well, enough said. But the same applies on down the line; a department head can make or mar that department. It must also be said that his ability to 'make' that department depends on the material at his disposal, in other words Old Able Seaman Jones or Stoker Smith, plus all the intervening personnel.

During my time on *Comus* I was lucky. I served under two skippers, both of whom would come under the heading of 'good uns'. The ship's company came and went, as was the routine of those days. The ships stayed on the Far East station ad-infinitum and crews were relieved piecemeal as their time came up. This was of course made worse by a percentage of the crew being conscripts, serving only eighteen months in total and you had them for about twelve months of that time. Just as they became useful to you they were gone – back to civilian life. But that is hardly their fault. The point emerging from this situation is that during nearly three years on this ship I must have served with around five hundred men. Bearing in mind that the ship's company was only a hundred and eighty, it illustrates the turn round of crew was prolific. Amongst them were 'good uns' and 'bad uns' and a myriad in between.

I joined *Comus* in Singapore fairly late in 1952 having taken passage on HMT *Dunera*.. A word about *Dunera* in passing. She was the 'Slow Boat to China' of her era. It took us about six weeks. Southampton to Singapore we were almost entirely full with service families, mainly army. I enjoyed that six weeks, probably in anticipation of life on a destroyer that I knew was to come. I subsequently met a lot of people who travelled with *Dunera* at some time or other and never heard a bad word about her.

There was a small contingent of naval personnel aboard, and my main work consisted of organizing them into keep-busy activities; conducted tours of the ship's engine room (diesel) and keep fit classes; the former with as high a technical content as possible, the latter as enjoyable as possible.

The Korean War was on at this time so no time was wasted in getting us back 'up there'. We left Singapore next morning up to Hong Kong; one night there, and on to Korea via another one night stop in Japan. Sasebo to be precise, which was at that time an American base; a good deep harbour which, prior to this period, had been one of Japan's larger naval bases.

An interesting and humorous story about Sasebo. It was my first time in Japan and I went ashore that night with a messmate who had been there before and knew what was what. The custom in bars was for the waitress, as she served you, to ask your name. Amazingly they seemed to remember all the names and after your first visit you would thereafter be called Mr John, Charley, or whatever your name was, on subsequent visits.

I was not aware of this and when the waitress asked our names my companion answered, before I could open my mouth, 'Eager and Willing, he's eager and I am willing.'

Well, it must have been six months or so before I put into Sasebo again. I went to the same bar and, as I opened the door to enter, the barman looked up and called, 'Why, hello Mr Eager, we haven't seen you for a long time.'

☆ ☆ ☆

What can be said about the Korean War? Not a lot, is the answer that comes to mind after all these years. After the war recently concluded it was a bit low key. The army had it rough, shoring up the Americans was a tough job in itself, but the navy really had a supporting role. I think I am right in saying that *Comus* was the only British ship that was hit, one boiler room wiped out.

One wonders why we ever fought over Korea? It was a matter of principle of course, and where would we be without it? As the previous paragraph infers, my opinion of the American forces was not terribly high, an opinion widely shared and endorsed by subsequent ignominious defeat in Vietnam. Man for man GI Joe was as good as most, but collectively something went wrong. Somehow the discipline that made other forces nigh invincible (one hesitates to name them) was somehow lacking in the Americans.

An experience on *Comus* illustrates this. There was an island off the west coast of Korea, well north of the fighting line at that time, held by American and south Korean troops. Its name escapes me but the obvious reason for holding it was strategic. It was an observation post and frequently used to mount nuisance raids and reconnaissance probes to the mainland. We conducted one of these raids and the composition of the force was surprising; amongst the Korean troops were children (male) of about thirteen in military uniform, but who changed into virtual rags on landing on the mainland, merged with the local populace and returned with all sorts of valuable information.

Because of its nuisance value, the north Koreans were very keen to eliminate this enemy stronghold but baulked at a frontal assault; instead they frequently tried clandestine landings and to combat this a UN destroyer used to slowly patrol the strait between mainland and island at night. This was an unpleasant task as on occasions it came under fire from both sides, foe and friend. One trick tried often was to float down on the tide, north to south, a barge laden with explosives. If it hit you, *good night!* But if it missed, they would collect it in the morning and tow it back to try again the next night. They couldn't lose.

This particular night *Comus* was on patrol and we picked up a vessel heading slowly and silently towards us. We challenged the vessel. No reply! A second challenge elicited a password, but it was the previous night's password. One more challenge and an unsatisfactory reply. We blew it out of the water. We had no alternative. A court of inquiry was held after it was revealed that said vessel was American on a mission to the mainland. No one thought to keep us informed. She went down with no survivors. The court of inquiry totally exonerated our skipper.

Another Korean War incident worthy of the telling was also on the west coast. The main railway ran along the coast for a couple of miles between two tunnels through the mountains, a very vulnerable point on the north Korean supply chain, in fact the only point at which that particular link could be attacked. It was in a shallow bay and we would regularly cruise into the bay unchallenged and lob four inch shells into the cliffs. The cliffs would crumble down and totally block the rail line. In effect this stoppage of supply only lasted a couple of weeks; hundreds of labourers would descend upon it and clear the blockage into the sea. We would then be requested by the army to help again and the whole operation would be repeated.

On this particular operation we again cruised leisurely into the bay, followed by a New Zealand frigate. We had just opened fire when a huge rail-mounted gun was trundled out of the tunnel at the south end and proceeded to answer back. To say we were surprised is to put it mildly; we were so used to cruising in, doing the job and cruising out. The first shot missed us by about three inches. It was probably nearer three yards, but I was on watch in the engine room at the time and, believe me, it felt like three inches. I swung open both turbine throttles and we literally 'leapt' out of the bay, almost ahead of the 'full speed ahead' showing on the telegraph. I was congratulated afterwards for my quick action, but my actions were motivated solely by the thought of self-preservation.

☆ ☆ ☆

Yokosuka and Sasebo in Japan were American naval bases at this time and Kure was the Commonwealth Force's base. You could be excused at times for thinking that you were in, say, San Diego in the case of the first two, and Aldershot or Portsmouth in the case of the latter. I was always aware that this was not the true Japan that I was seeing, so whenever possible I got away by train or bus to see the real thing. Visits to Hiroshima were an education; the city was very slowly recovering from the atom bomb. The place was still in the main flattened, but the road and rail links were by now reopened and it was possible to visualize things as they were a few years previously and to peruse their resurrection. At even this period after the explosion people were still dropping dead in the streets from the after-effects.

So much has been said and written on the subject of that first atomic explosion that I do not propose to elaborate on the subject. But even now I am conscious of the fact that I am one of a relatively small percentage of the world's population that had actually seen the effects of an atomic explosion.

My personal relationships with the Japanese were good. So soon after 1945, the general feeling was the Chinese were the goodies and the Japanese the baddies. My own experiences did not reflect that. To my knowledge I was never 'seen off' by a Japanese but to quote a cliché, the Chinese would 'pinch the sugar out of your tea.'

I will tell a story that will illustrate my opinion. In Kure a colleague in the Australian navy invited me to his 'local' for a couple of bottles one evening. 'Just hop in a tri-taxi,' he said, 'and ask for the Mona bar.' Tri-taxis plied outside the dock gates by the dozen, so it was not necessary to obtain further details of location. The custom was to agree the fare before commencing the journey; accordingly I asked the driver, 'How much to the Mona bar?' Two hundred yen was the agreed figure (about four shillings, or 20p if you are that young).

We drove into town and stopped outside the Ramona Bar. I was about to alight when I noticed the error and pointed it out to the driver who scratched his head in perplexity. We then toured the town looking for the Mona. No joy. We stopped and asked two different policemen on point duty, who also expressed perplexity. Next stop was the taxi depot; maps were studied, guides were consulted, no joy. So we headed for the road again, but just as we were about to leave the depot another driver was coming in. He was consulted almost as a last despairing attempt. Smiles on both sides. Both drivers beamed and off we went armed with newly acquired knowledge. We drove out of town along the Inland Sea coast road towards Hiroshima. A couple of miles and we stopped at an entrance to a narrow alley and there down this dark unprepossessing thoroughfare was a dim neon sign proclaiming that this was at last, Mona's Bar.

I had been in that cab around an hour and wondered how much the bill would be. 'Two hundred yen,' said the driver, 'that was agreed and if I couldn't find it that was my fault, not yours.' Can you imagine that in London? Paris? New York? Anywhere?

The Japanese are a complex race. The atrocities of the world war should never be forgotten and by the writer never will be. But meeting them afterwards, well you would never believe them to be of the same culture.

One good habit of theirs we could well adopt is the hot towel in restaurants and bars. Before even ordering in a respectable restaurant, a small hand towel is brought to you in a metal dish straight from a steamer, to freshen face and hands after the dusty streets.

On the sporting front there is a humorous story to tell. *Comus* had a good football team, in fact a very good football team by Far East standards of the period. On one visit to

HMS *Comus*, Okinawa, 1954

Yokosuka we were challenged by the American base team. They said to us, 'We realize we have a temerity to challenge you, your reputation has preceded you, but we have only just started soccer and want to learn the game. Who better to learn from than yourselves.' We accepted the challenge and the game was on. I think we approached it with a certain amount of arrogance. That is the only excuse I can offer for what happened.

We were first on the field and when they followed we couldn't believe our eyes. They all had the same shirts, but they also wore Palm Beach shorts, and no two pairs were the same colour. They were all well over six foot tall and intimidating, all ex-grid iron footballers. I won't bore the reader with details, but we never settled at all – a combination possibly of our arrogance and their intimidation. The end result was 2-0 to them! It took a long time to live that defeat down; it was rubbed in wherever sport was discussed in service circles, in Hong Kong and Singapore.

The surviving members of the HMS *Comus* football team, 35 years on, at their reunion in Portsmouth, 1991.

To have an evening ashore in Japan at that time required a degree of financial acumen. You see the Far East Fleet base, as far as accounting was concerned, was Singapore, and accordingly we were paid in Straits dollars, each worth 2s. 4d. (11p). This was invariably changed into Hong Kong dollars 1s. 3d. (6p) as the most used currency. But on setting foot in Japan, if you used the British Service Clubs you would need British occupation money in sterling. If you used any of the American clubs you needed American occupation money, Script dollars they were called. Then, of course, you needed yen in Japanese establishments (1,000 per £).

Thank goodness for the designers of our uniforms. I have frequently gone ashore with five different currencies in five different pockets and a mind boggled by the complexities.

Altogether, Japan was an experience. The Far East generally was a good experience, but I think Japan lingers in the memory longer than a lot of other places. Why? Well it was so different to our own way of life. By this time I had been at sea for thirteen years and had seen a lot of places, but Japan was so different from anywhere else. We must have entered Japanese ports thirty times in that period.

☆ ☆ ☆

About Malaya and Singapore: Hardly was the conflict in Korea over (it was over on paper but still lingered on in reality) than the communist insurgence in Malaya was hotting up, and we found ourselves Singapore-based as part of the anti-communist force on the mainland. Once again our role was in support of the army and once again they bore the brunt. But the amount of co-operation was above expectation. We occasionally joined the army on jungle patrols whilst in dock, all voluntarily. The army thought we were totally mad to volunteer for such duties, and who can deny it? I even found myself as Commanding Officer of a train on several occasions, and if you can think of a more unlikely occupation for a sailor I would like to hear of it. Remember that during the emergency all trains were controlled by the military and run as military operations. Civilians needed a permit before being able to purchase a ticket.

Following the rigours of the Korean campaign, *Comus* was

due for dry docking for a short refit, so as soon as we came south, this was carried out in a Singapore dockyard. The ship's company moved into the base, HMS *Terror*. It took three months as I remember. After destroyer life, living ashore in an establishment like *Terror* was pure heaven. Sleeping in beds – unheard of luxury, good food (well better food anyway), every sports facility one could think of, mess life and on the other side of the island, Singapore city.

I remember this period primarily I think for the sport. *Comus* was a respected, highly respected, force in practically every sport. It happened all too infrequently that quite by coincidence, luck, call it what you will, one particular ship would be blessed with a strong sporting crew; success breeds success and you soon have a situation where even modest performers exceed themselves and are fighting for places in teams. *Comus* at this time was such a ship. Crew members came and went, but the overall standard was maintained. For a ship's company of only around a hundred and eighty, we worked wonders.

I had the honour to captain the soccer team for most of this period, until towards the end injuries to my left leg gave me no alternative but to call it a day. But to stick to the Malay period, we played pretty well everyone – civilian clubs, army, RAF, and other naval units. We didn't lose too many, and when you think of RAF Seletor for example, whose manpower was around 10,000, well I think we had justification for pride. The *apres*-game atmosphere was great too, particularly after playing an army outfit. Army hospitality has always been tops in my estimation and long lasting friendships emerged from such gatherings.

One such event well remembered, took place in Port Dickson. We spent four days anchored there about a mile off, over an Easter weekend. I took one look at the place on emerging from the engine room and decided that was all I wanted to see of it. But fate intervened, we received a signal from the Malay Regiment, whose depot was just outside the town, challenging us that evening at football.

The challenge was duly accepted and army transport was laid on for us. The first person I set eyes on was a sergeant major I had last seen in Singapore months before, and in the intervening period he had acquired the post of Barrack Master to the Malay Regiment. So instead of spending a boring weekend on board, I spent a great weekend with Terry, wife and daughter at their villa, with its own beach. Swimming by day, mess social life by evening. It did not finish there; whilst strolling along the beach one afternoon, we ran into another army man with wife, whom I had known in Penang and Singapore, in service boxing circles. He was a mutual friend and was enjoying a spot of leave in Port Dickson.

As to the match itself, it was relatively uneventful. I think we won 2-1, but I came away with one of those everlasting memories that life is all about. Because the Malay Regiment was predominantly Moslem, no after-match entertainment in the conventional style was possible, so an English sergeant instructor organized a long galvanised bath full with bottles of beer, topped with blocks of ice, on the touchline immediately after the final whistle. About five hundred people watched the game, around seventy from *Comus*. We all drifted towards the bath, the English that is, but after our first thirst was slaked we had hardly dented the supply of bottles and, as we started to drift away towards our transport, the said sergeant looked at all the beer left over, drew himself to his full height, puffed out his chest and roared in true British army fashion 'Nobody leaves 'ere till orl this beer's gorn.' Didn't have much choice did we?

It was rare at this time for enough of HM ships to be in the same place at the same time to set up any sort of sporting competition. But an exception occurred during our docking spell in Singapore. HMS *Constance* came in for about a week; deadly rivalry existed between us and no time was lost in setting up a sporting marathon. We played one another at everything, soccer, cricket, hockey, rugby, you name it! Yes even darts and yes even golf. All designed to include pretty well all of both ship's companies. The points were totted up as each event was concluded, bets were made (quietly) and on the last day, the day before *Constance* sailed, it all depended upon the soccer match.

That morning the heavens opened and it rained as it can only rain in the tropics; by noon the pitch was under several inches of water, but that game was going to be played if we all drowned in the process. Kick-off was at 1600. A very important element manifested itself at this moment. The

Queen had been on a visit to Australia and on her way home in the royal yacht, passed through our waters and in the time honoured tradition she ordered 'Splice the Mainbrace' to the Far East Fleet. This extra rum ration was made at 1600.

When the game started both ships' companies were lined up on each side of the pitch, baying for blood. Rangers and Celtic on New Year's Day! You ain't seen nothing. The result of the match? Almost seems coincidental doesn't it? Oh yes, we won, and with it the Victor Ludorum or whatever it was. Memories are made of this!

My other interest in the sporting scene was boxing and I had a small team in training on *Comus*. In most ships in which I served, boxing was my own personal preserve. I always managed a small team with whatever talent was available. I didn't do too bad on *Comus*. I had one or two useful talents although opportunities to show them had been few and far between.

But during this spell in Singapore I also had under my wing two young civilian lads aged eighteen and fourteen, the sons of an Admiralty intelligence officer. An association continued during my whole Far East tour, on and off, as permitted by circumstances. We had gym facilities under their bungalow; other kids joined in, European and Asian, and we enjoyed some local success. Both lads represented Singapore on boxing tours of Australia and Thailand. Sonny Chia I remember well from this period. He was professional Orient featherweight champion and in his spare time he trained the Singapore Harbour Board Boys Club. A great guy and so modest.

I met a lot of 'characters' in the boxing field at this time. One such was a prominent member of the Singapore government, a Eurasian gentleman of high repute. He was also President of the local Amateur Boxing Association, that is how we met. He came over to me at a tournament in Jahore Bahru and congratulated me on the improvement shown by the two brothers. From that moment, no matter which bar or similar establishment I went into, whether alone or with friends, this venerable character was always to be found ensconced in a corner, usually a dark corner, and a drink appeared in front of me almost before I had time to sit, ordered and paid for by said gentleman. Gentleman? Yes, who could deny that epitaph to someone who buys you a drink on sight over a period of years. Although our connection was only through sport, we met again in the boxing world when he ran the Jahore Bahru Boys Club and his thirteen year old son was in the boxing section.

There is one more character I must introduce to you at this juncture. Tom was a public hangman, and there are not too many of those around. Tom is not his real name, but I use it to protect his anonimity and those still living.

His was quite a story. During the war he was a paratrooper and was part of the force that reoccupied Singapore after the Japanese surrender. He hadn't been there long when, as has happened a million times, he met a fair damsel, though in this case a dusky damsel – a charming Eurasian girl. They eventually married and when he returned to the UK she came with him, but she just could not adjust to the English climate; the first winter she was very ill, and after the second winter in which she nearly died doctors told Tom that she would not survive another one and if he valued her life to get her back into the climatic zone to which she was accustomed. He had left the army by this time and was a prison warder. This stood him in good stead and he obtained a post, through the Colonial Office, as a prison warder in the notorious Changi Jail, now, of course, again a civilian jail.

Some years later there was a vacancy to transfer to the mainland prison service at Jahore, with a nice bungalow just outside the prison walls, to go with it. Application was made and quickly approved, and the transition made. On Tom's first day some reference was made in the mess about 'you wait till your first topping.' It then emerged that 'topping' was the responsibility of the junior officer, something that had not emerged at the interview. Remember that the Malayan terrorist campaign was at its height then. Hanging was the penalty for terrorism and it took place very frequently, once or perhaps twice a week. The ropes came out from England, ready for use, so all the 'topper' had to do was to operate the trap. All he had to do?

It was with fear and trepidation that Tom approached his first job, but by the time I knew him he was completely inured to it and he reckoned his family's holidays were financed by the 'toppings'. 'Going up to Penang in a couple of month's,' he would say, 'should get in enough toppings by then.'

On the days when this occurred he would be called early, the deed was always done at dawn, took his wife in a cup of tea, then off to work. The bungalow was so close to the prison wall that she could hear the trap sprung and then would get up and cook his breakfast, knowing he would be home as soon as the doctor declared the body deceased. Tom then had the day off, plus the cash bonus at the end of the month.

I got to know the family fairly well, and liked them all, and as a result of this was at their residence one evening, and was invited into the prison for a look round. There was to be an execution due the following dawn and all the prisoners then interned were banging their tea mugs on the bars and chanting communist slogans endlessly. This would continue all night, rising into a crescendo at dawn. Then as the trap was heard to operate, silence. A deep eerie, frightening silence. It was uncanny, particularly when the only people that were supposed to know of the impending execution were the Governor, the Padre and the 'topper.' But they always did know. Somehow!

I referred earlier to train journeys through Malaya. During my time there I had a couple of spells of local leave and took advantage of the army leave centre on Penang Island. The centre was army administered, bar catering by NAAFI, social events by WVS. One doesn't tend to think of the WVS in terms of the Malayan jungle, but they did a great job. I remember one afternoon looking at, in passing, two WVS girls giving ballroom dancing lessons to about twenty-five young soldiers in jungle greens and jungle boots. All were wet through with perspiration and the boots were being wielded without much precision. Boy, did those girls earn their pay? Such as it was, I enjoyed those spells in Penang. It was a beautiful tropical island, beautiful tropical beaches, good food and drink and good company. What more could one ask of a leave?

There had to be a price to pay, there always is, isn't there? That price was the journey up there and back. We would start in the early morning from Singapore and would take all day to get to Kuala Lumpur; a couple of hours break, then the night train to Prai, ferry over to Georgetown on the island, then by road. It took the next day to get over the journey. With terrorist attacks in mind, the train could not travel faster than it could come to a halt if it suddenly found progress impeded by a felled tree across the line; so unless there was a long straight stretch ahead progress could be mighty slow.

Being a military operation, a Commanding Officer was appointed for each journey and it was always the senior man, all services, below a certain level. I don't know what that level was but I always found myself in charge. This involved organizing said 'all services' into watches for sentry duty and then saying a silent prayer that the terrorists had a night off on that journey. On one trip there were some Gurkhas aboard and their sergeant said to me, 'My men will guard the train, your men can sleep.' I slept well that night in the knowledge that no train was ever better guarded.

We were actually attacked by the communists on one journey going north. I won't go into the details but would refer the reader to Leslie Thomas's book *The Virgin Soldiers,* in which he describes an attack. The only thing I would disagree with him about is that it wasn't funny. He made an extremely humorous situation out of it, but it is not so funny when it happens to you! However, we managed to spring the ambush without losing any blood. Can't say the same for our adversaries though.

There was one more sporting activity I tried my hand at in this period. Tug-of-War! One of my POs had some considerable experience at the sport, coaching some good crews, so whilst the facilities existed at HMS *Terror* we availed ourselves of them.

The facilities were excellent and consisted of two tall trees about six feet apart, adapted with the aid of wire strops and a system of pulleys, one three feet above ground level and the other about fifteen feet above. You pulled the rope which then went through the pulleys and down to the metal tray on the other side which could be loaded with large lumps of pig iron. Training was done in the cool of the morning, usually around 0500. Got to be keen to do that, haven't you?

The proof of the pudding, as the saying goes, came with the Singapore Open Championships. I can't remember how many entries there were, but we came through and won. The final against the police team turned into an anti-climax for yours truly; after battling through all the stages, my left knee, the one injured at football, let me down and I had to be replaced. No medal!

Our team consisted of seven big seamen and stokers, plus me. Coach said my build was ideal for number one, short and thick; from the neck downwards he hastened to add.

Before closing, I would say a word about social life in Singapore itself. It is well documented that social life was on a high plane in the colony, and mine was well taken care of through sporting acquaintances. The father of the two lads previously referred to looked after me rather well, as some recompense for my efforts I imagine. I met a lot of people and a lot of doors were open to me that would not have been otherwise open had it not been for sporting achievements. It was a relatively small European community and fame, however slight, tended to spread quickly.

☆ ☆ ☆

I suppose after Singapore, we spent more time based in Hong Kong than anywhere else. Not unnaturally, it was a large naval base with dockyard facilities. It was a popular base, everyone enjoyed time in Hong Kong. Whatever your tastes in life, they could be indulged in Hong Kong. Including good sporting facilities. Here we go again!

Once again I was fortunate with contacts, with some good friends, mostly army. One family was very good to me and I stayed with them regularly when in port. I also had friends in the Welsh Regiment and Royal Ulster Rifles. The former, well their bandmaster, shared my cabin on the *Dunera,* already referred to. I still remember Sunday 'tiffin' times at their mess up on the Chinese border. Hic!

The Royal Ulster Rifles were an outfit I had a lot of time for. After the Far East I seemed to bump into them all over the world, including during the emergency in Cyprus. A greater crowd it is difficult to imagine, and their loyalty to the Crown, second to none. That should never be forgotten, particularly in the light of current politics.

A tale that must be told and I sincerely hope I am not betraying any army secrets here! On St Patrick's Night someone from the RUR, wild horses wouldn't get me to reveal who, broke into the Welsh Regiment lines, sought out the Regimental mascot, a goat who rejoiced in the name of Taffy (I think he was the fourteenth of that ilk) and painted him green. Then made his getaway undetected. Consternation is the word that fitted the Welsh reaction to the incident. It was obvious from the colour paint used, and the date, who was responsible. Retaliatory action was planned and I understand only the intervention of the two COs concerned stopped this from happening. I was told years later, admittedly by a soldier with his tongue well embedded in his cheek, that the man responsible was duly promoted, for showing daring and initiative.

Just prior to this incident I was present when poor old Taffy thoroughly disgraced himself. It was the occasion of the St David's Day Regimental Ball at the Peninsular Hotel, Kowloon. The participants in the ceremony of the 'Eating of the Leek' were duly lined up on the ballroom floor, leek in one hand, pint of beer in the other. Taffy was stood to attention with his escort. Drums rolled. You're way ahead of me aren't you? Yes, Taffy misbehaved himself in the middle of the floor.

Football was very strong in Hong Kong and once again we enjoyed considerable success. On one occasion we played Hong Kong Football Club and only lost to them narrowly. Now the said HKFC was far and away the best in the Far East. Remember this was prior to the emergence of Korea and China as premier soccer playing countries. When you think of the number of potential players they could draw from compared to our one hundred and eighty men in total, I think we stood tall.

Another sporting occasion that stood out, in my memory anyway, was in opposition to the Gurkhas. We were anchored for a couple of days in Junk Bay, in the New Territories, and received an invitation to spend a day with them and clash with them at soccer, hockey and basketball. They supplied transport up to the Chinese border and battle duly commenced. They beat us at hockey, but we won the other two. Highly competitive games all of them, but fair, no quarter asked and none given.

After the sporting confrontations they took advantage of us. Perhaps you will have heard of the Gurkha appetite for rum. At that time they received a liberal ration of the stuff and seemed to consume it as we consume beer. We were not unused to the beverage but no way could we compete with them. I found out why they are such good fighters; with that amount of rum in me I would take on the world and his brother.

Our skipper, a member of the hockey team, was dined by their CO. I was guest of the WO's mess, then after dining we joined up with the rest of our teams and that is when the rum started to flow, and flow, and flow. The return journey was quite an event in itself. We were due back in Junk Bay about 2100 where our boats were waiting. I think it was about 0100 when we got there. The skipper had a staff car for transport. I had a jeep, and the best of the deal, the fresh air rushing past did wonders for my head; but the lads were in army trucks and to describe the scene when we arrived at the jetty is beyond my limited literary propensity. It is best left to the reader's imagination anyway!

We liked the Gurkhas, great guys! Some weeks after the episode we were going out from Hong Kong on a one day exercise and invited a party of them along for the ride. They thoroughly enjoyed themselves, I think. It was always hard to tell, with their inscrutable faces, their looks never betrayed their emotions. I wonder if they still receive their rum ration? I hope so! It is difficult in my mind to imagine them without it.

Over the years I had several attempts at boat pulling. Not rowing, definitely not! An instructor in my early navy days described rowing as something you did on the lake, Sunday afternoons with the girlfriend. Boat pulling could not have been further from that. A five man crew in a whaler in an open sea, hard thwarts to sit on, no sliding seats, no foot rests. I don't remember the length of the oars, but they were mighty long and mighty heavy. Boat pulling is a real man's sport.

It reared its ugly head again in Hong Kong. The whole Far East Fleet was due to assemble in Junk Bay and with some months notice a fleet regatta was arranged. A regatta consisted of about ten races, seamen of each ship competing against seamen, stokers v stokers and so on, all over eight cables. But the speciality was the 'open' - the number one crew from each ship, all ranks, racing over twelve cables. Once again being short and stocky made me an ideal 'mid boat' man at number three. It was considered an honour to make the open team. I viewed it as such.

Training was conducted in great secrecy, pre-dawn in the harbour, so that rivals could not see. At sea, skippers took great delight in dropping a crew, then steaming ahead for a couple of miles, I feel it was nearer five miles at times, and then you had to catch up. It was disconcerting in the South China Sea when at times your ship would disappear from view in the swell and you could not see where you were going. We did fairly well overall in the regatta, but I am sad to say my crew did not win.

The foregoing about Hong Kong might give the impression that life was all sports and social. Not so. This was the period of confrontation between Chinese communists on the mainland and nationalists on Formosa, now Taiwan. British Merchant shipping about its legal business was entitled to Royal Navy protection in the Formosa straits and that is where we came in. It was fraught with peril, frequently again we were shelled from both sides. War is difficult enough when you don't know who your enemy is; extremely difficult when you are not allowed to fire back.

China coast typhoons! Just the mere phrase conjures up terror at sea and mountainous waves. They were the other hazard of serving in these waters. We experienced three during this period. In two our involvement was only peripheral, but the other one hit Hong Kong like a bombshell. We were actually at sea at the time, which was lucky for us. With a small ship you just stick your nose into it and concentrate on staying where you are. The engine speed involved should be giving you about twenty knots, but in fact you are not moving. Just to stay upright and alive is your sole objective. We spent five days like that with no food other than hard-tack, ship's biscuits with the consistency of chipboard. Sleep was just not possible and washing and other ablutions out of the question. Hour after hour, day after day, life was a survival exercise. But when it was over, a day or so to recover, into Hong Kong and life became good again.

I mentioned it was lucky we were at sea as the typhoon struck. To stay in harbour was plain suicide as you would be dashed against the dock walls, probably to destruction. On this occasion one ship was in dry dock when the typhoon warning came. There was a panic to get her undocked and lorries toured the area picking up dock workers to get her watertight and out. She made it to open sea just in time. When the elements struck, the dry dock caisson was wrecked and so too would have been the ship, had she still been there.

On the subject of docking, we developed an underwater fault in the Formosa Straits and signalled Hong Kong with desperate need to dock. They replied that this was out of the question, but to proceed to a small Chinese yard where facilities had been made available. I don't know where it was, the area was so remote, but we did get a good job done. The surprising thing was that although the work force was Chinese, the management at all levels was Scottish. We met them socially in the evenings and they were so glad to see us.

One last humorous tale about Hong Kong that must be recounted. I spent my last Christmas (of three) in the Far East with an army family. They had three young daughters and consequently tried to make Christmas as much as it would have been at home as possible. They managed that pretty well with one exception. They could not get a Christmas tree. The evening of 24 December we had been to the mess, had a drink or two and on return were sitting leisurely on the balcony. My eyes casually alighted on a large plantation of conifers across a valley in the far distance. My host saw them simultaneously. We looked at one another and said, 'Why not?'

We set off carrying a saw. The valley was much further away than we had anticipated. It turned out to be a monsoon gully about ten feet wide and six feet deep and it took some navigating, but we made it, and up the hills to the trees. We found one about the right size, cut it down and commenced the return journey. What had been a hazardous journey empty handed was doubly so with a tree to manhandle, particularly the gully. Eventually we got back to the quarters about 0700, when the sun was in the sky, to find we could not get the tree into the lift. Neither could we negotiate the bends when we tried the stairs. Out into the court we got busy with the saw and got the thing to manageable proportions. Finally, into the lift and in the apartment. My host's wife was almost berserk wondering what could have happened. We sank into armchairs and slept most of Christmas Day. But the children had their tree.

There was conjecture afterwards as to whether we had actually crossed the Chinese border on our expedition, an unpardonable sin at that period. If it was so I can only thank whatever or whoever was guiding us up there.

☆ ☆ ☆

Now for British North Borneo (Sabah) and for clarity's sake I will include Sarawak and Brunei in this part of the story. We did not spend long there, only about two weeks in total, but it was a trip packed with incident one way or another.

I suppose the story starts with an act of piracy. One tends to think this happened only in the last century, but not so; in the period of which I am writing, piracy was rife in this part of the world, hard vicious and extremely cruel piracy. They were mainly Philipinos and very difficult to catch. They plied their trade in old Chinese junks, old by appearance anyway. When chased they would clutch in extremely powerful diesel engines and disappear over the horizon in a cloud of dust, as the saying goes.

This particular incident involved a small isolated village miles up a creek on the east coast of BNB. The people fed off the land and the jungle, and harvested copra in a small godown (warehouse). The only contact they had with the outside world was when twice a year a trading junk came up the creek and took their copra in return for other goods, tinned food, drink and cloth for making clothing. An idyllic way of life. Then came the day they knew the trading junk was about due. It appeared, they thought, making its way slowly up the creek under sail. Preparations were made to welcome it. Remember it only happened twice a year. Probably a pig was killed and prepared in order to make their guests happy. A feast day!

But tragedy was about to shatter their world. As the junk came alongside the frail wooden jetty the crew leapt ashore and revealed their true identity. Pirates. They stole the total copra crop, making the villagers load the junk under the threat of rifles. They stole everything they could lay hands on, of even remote value, and put the village to the torch. As a final gesture they took a couple of the more shapely girls on to the junk who were 'crew raped' and then thrown, almost lifeless on to the jetty. A few males resisted, but were quickly shot and dumped into the creek. The junk then sailed off down the creek leaving a totally devastated community.

When the shock wore off a little, a 'runner' was dispatched to the nearest village where telegraph facilities existed and the news communicated to the capital, Sandakan, which relayed same to Singapore. All this must have taken a week by which time the miscreants were heaven knows where. Enter *Comus* upon the scene. We were in Singapore, just about to embark upon a football tour of BNB, Sarawak and Brunei. We had to shove off at short notice, find the creek, find the village and do what we could, which was not a lot. The local District Officer joined us before we entered the creek; his liaison was vital, not merely for language difficulties, but advising on what to expect and how to handle the situation. As I said, we did what we could, and they were genuinely pleased to see us.

A hastily arranged football match was organized on their Padang, or clearing. We landed a very scratch team and a good time was had by all; half our opponents played without footwear. I refereed this one and contrived to make it a draw, a really diplomatic result that. I felt quite proud of myself. It meant denying *Comus* a perfectly justifiable penalty in the closing seconds, but everyone was delighted. I feel sure upon reflection that they really thought they had drawn with England.

It took about eight hours of skillful navigating to get a ship of our size up that creek, but the next night we had a young rating go sick with appendicitis and he needed urgent surgery. We got back in about four hours to a mission hospital at the mouth of the creek. If getting in was good navigation by day, getting out by night in half that time was super navigation. When we got to the hospital we were met by an ancient Scottish nurse-in-charge and informed that the doctor was 'away on his rounds' and was not expected back for three weeks. But she knew exactly what was required and did it.

We were off then to resume our football tour. We played five games in six days, at Lahad Datu, Sandakan, Miri and Kuala Belait. Four won and one drawn. The first one in Sandakan was the 'biggie' on a Saturday against the Capital Select. One rather strange memory of the crowd at that game: there was a large stand on one side of the ground holding several thousand, but when we kicked off a total of around fifty people we thought, so much for our drawing power. But as the whistle went, all shops and businesses in the town closed down, and all the males of all ages came to the match. There must have been about five thousand in total.

The last match of the tour at Miri was against Shell Oil; a very large field there (oil that is) with wonderful sporting facilities; a truly international team too, comprising English, Chinese, Malays and the captain and goalkeeper was a Dutch international. The referee was from Cheshire.

Following the game there was a 'do' at the club, and what a wonderful evening! Towards the end, the Cheshire referee weaved his way towards me and said, 'I would like you and your two friends (non-playing members) to come home with me for a meal and meet the family. Come on, I have a jeep outside.' I think the jeep knew its own way home, otherwise we would not have arrived. It was jungle road that deteriorated into a track and how we missed the trackside trees is beyond me. However, we pulled up outside a beautiful bungalow, one of several company residences in a compound. His wife, an Australian girl, made us welcome and went into the kitchen to prepare steak and vegetables. She had no idea we were coming and servants had long since gone home. It took an hour or two but she produced a lovely meal.

All this time, us four males sat around talking in front of the drinks cabinet, which was considerably depleted as time went by.

By the time she served the meal, one of my shipmates was flat out on the settee and the other looked at the food and turned green. Our host said, 'I don't think I am hungry dear.' She looked at me as much as to say, 'You dare!' Manfully, or was it through fear, I sat at the table and consumed a meal. I often wondered subsequently what she said to him after he returned from taking us back to the jetty. Men have been divorced for less.

Altogether a memorable trip was Borneo.

☆ ☆ ☆

The rest of the Far East: sounds a vast subject doesn't it? Well of course it is. When you think of the countries involved and the area covered it is a big subject. Indonesia, the Philippines, Fiji, New Guinea, Northern Australia, Ceylon (as it was then) and India. Also a million (or so it seemed at the time) islands, mostly very beautiful but, from the point of view of this epistle, fairly uneventful.

One possible exception was Manus Island in the Admiralty Island group. The Australian Navy had a base there and we were their guests. During the war, and during the American advance northwards, they established an air base on the island, abandoning it totally as the push north decreed, including a few aircraft unserviceable at the time. In the intervening years the jungle had reasserted itself. Trees, vines and creepers had crept up through the buildings, planes, vehicles and totally overtaken them. In the jungle silence, an eerie experience.

An amusing adjunct to the Manus Island visit. Whilst we were sitting on a tropical beach admiring the scenery, two native islanders emerged from the jungle, clad in just loin sarongs and gazed at us in amazement. Our amazement was at least equal to theirs, I might add. A friend took a snap of them and when I sent a copy home to the family, their comment was, 'Nice photograph, but who is that with you?' Mind you, I had been away about two years this time.

The Far East experience as a whole? It was tough at times, but it was new to me and altogether an experience I would not have missed. But I was glad to get home. The passage back to the UK was aboard HMT *Devonshire,* Hong Kong to Liverpool, seven weeks. It was a leisurely voyage, enjoyable after the rigours of destroyer life.

4

Far East Aftermath
1955-1958

Three years, in fact three years and three months. In the preceding writings, that period of time took in so many happenings, so much travelling, so much experience. But the tale to tell over these years won't take very long.

All my naval career to date had been at sea, with the exception of the study period just after the war; all of it active, extremely active, but now I got a break.

Being in the engine room department meant that the chances of a shore-side job were pretty remote; there were just not that many to be had. Other branches were more fortunate; the clerical department, the Fleet Air Arm for example spent a proportionally large part of their time ashore and to go to sea must have been a change for them. But when I did get a shore job, I got a good one. In fact in my branch it was the best job in the navy. Getting it was pure chance, nothing to do with skill or influence, just being in the right place at the right time.

By this time I was a Chief Mechanician. Purely by coincidence the job of Regulating Chief Mechanician was about to become vacant. All the other available candidates had been home for some time and we were near the top of the roster for foreigns, all except lucky me. See what I mean by being in the right place at the right time? By virtue of my position I was the senior Ch./Mech. in the Portsmouth division and, Portsmouth being the senior depot, I was the senior Ch./Mech. in the navy.

We lived at Waterlooville at this time, then a delightful little village at the back of the downs about eight miles north of Portsmouth. Life was good. I almost forgot what a ship looked like. Well almost. My office was in the RN barracks, so it was only on rare occasions that I ventured into the dockyard.

On the sporting scene, there was not a lot happening. I watched Pompey occasionally, as I had done for years when the opportunity presented itself. And I did take another step in the boxing world. I thought it was time to move in a different direction, so I took exams and became a referee and judge. There were plenty of opportunities to practise and hone one's skills in this field, in and around Portsmouth. Being the premier naval port, there was a lot of activity during a season, from novices' competitions to Imperial Services Championships involving all three services. The standard was high too. National service was still on and good class boxers were available whilst doing their stint. I carried on as an 'official' in the sport for the rest of my time in the service.

The social side of the job was much more active. I was involved in mess life and all the social functions that entailed. For example, when foreign fleets visited Portsmouth, all sorts of social functions would be arranged, including 'a bit of a do' in the mess for equivalent ranks of the visitors. This was something we were required to do, an obligation, not just a necessity, a gesture of good feeling. Having said that, these occasions were invariably great, a good time being had by all. I remember entertaining Poles, Canadians, Americans, Russians and many more. The Russians were here on the occasion of the controversial Buster Crabbe episode.

We had at this time an Irish barman in the mess who instituted a Spastic penny pile on the counter. He would give change in pennies if possible, then shame you into adding them to his pile. There came the time very quickly when the pile reached the top of the bar. We called in the local spastics people and told them we wanted to break the pile at a forthcoming mess do and would they have a representative present to count the money, issue a receipt, and take it away. The total came to £120, that was an awful lot of 'old' pennies. They were most grateful and suggested that we try to get a celebrity of some sort to do the honours. That way they said the local press would become interested and we would get some good publicity for our efforts and they would get publicity as well. After some thought it was decided to write to Wilfred Pickles and ask him. This was done, but the answer was something of a let down. 'Delighted,' he said, 'and my fee will be 100 guineas.' After telling him where to go we decided to ask Frankie Howerd, who was appearing in a summer show at the Kings Theatre, Southsea. At least his expenses would be less, we reasoned. His response was refreshing; he not only declined any fee, but made a further contribution to the fund. He came straight from the theatre on a Saturday night.

We decided to match his graciousness with some of our own. He was escorted to the barracks by motor cycle outriders in uniform. We had to obtain Commodore's approval to do this and the local police had to be involved. Both parties were delighted to assist and entered into the spirit of things. Police were stationed at strategic points en route to facilitate an easy run. Frankie was taken into the mess office on arrival and given a glass of rum. 'You're trying to get me drunk,' he said, 'you sailors are all the same.' He then went out and gave lots of patter, then broke the penny pile. Frankie Howerd came out of the episode very high in my estimation, and has remained so.

I would add a tribute here to the generosity of the matelot when it came to charity. Every ship I served on had a favourite charity and money would be raised by many and devious means. As soon as the kitty was in a reasonable state a cheque would be sent off. Spastics were a perennial as was Great Ormond Street Children's Hospital. Sometimes I feel I have shares in the latter, so much was raised over the years.

And so drew to a conclusion a very enjoyable period of my naval life. Soon it would be back to sea, all too soon; but I had acquired a certain amount of sanity, if that is the right word during this time, a certain slowing down. Mind you my waist line was a little more padded, due to the soft civilian style life, but I had no doubt it would resume its more normal proportions once I was a destroyer man again.

There is one more tale to tell, appropriate at this juncture. I have referred to our Irish barman. Well after the *Naiad* was lost in 1942, it was the destroyer *Jervis* that picked me out of the water, and I said many times over the intervening years that I would love to meet someone who had been on the *Jervis* at that time to express my gratitude in some tangible form. I had known Mick the barman for years. I knew he had been in the navy during the war, but we had never got down to discussing details. One day in conversation it emerged that he was a member of the *Jervis* crew at that time. The only one I ever met. We did enjoy a pint or two that day, and one or two more over the next year or so.

I wonder what happened to Mick? He probably works for the big NAAFI in the sky now. I wonder if he organizes penny piles for charity up there?

5

The Home/Med.
1958-1961

HMS *Armada* D14 was a destroyer of the battle class, a bit larger than the CO/CH class, but not too dissimilar. I was able to fit into this, my next appointment, reather easily. I was really pleased about that after three years ashore.

Three years when what you stood on didn't move around; then all of a sudden it did, but one soon adapts to it. Altogether in retrospect, although there were a few

HMS *Armada*, 1958-1960, during Cyprus campaign

disappointments, this was another good commission. We certainly covered some ground, well water actually, but you know what I mean. We achieved a lot too, I felt, in the trouble spots of the day. Cyprus and then the so called Cod War.

By this time my football playing days were about over, but I still had the boxing interest. I had a few lads under training but did not achieve anything you will find in the record books. However, it was enjoyable. I also officiated from time to time, but another sporting interest reared its head. One of my Petty Officers was a fanatical athlete, taking part in long and middle distance stuff and frequently road races. He talked me into doing some training spins with him.

It became a regular thing and I became keen enough to acquire a new track suit and shoes. The funny thing was that after four mile spins he would return to the ship, shower and go to bed, whereas I would shower and go ashore for a quiet beer. I was nearing forty by now, and figured I had earned a pint. The trouble was, he was two years older than me. He put me to shame.

But back to business. By now foreign commissions had been reduced from two-and-a-half years to one-and-a-half years. A progressive step, but my experience was it usually took three years to do your two-and-a-half, and so it was with me on *Armada*. It took me well over two years to do my one-and-a-half. When I see in the press today that a ship has been away for six months and is accorded a hero's welcome on return, it makes me think I was born too soon.

My wife nearly went berserk whilst watching television during the Falklands battle, seeing naval wives complaining that they had not seen their husbands for three months. I try not to get bitter about it when I look at the pensions they get today, and their total time in action is counted in *days,* and compare it with my own!

I joined *Armada* in Rosyth and we shoved off next morning for Germany; Cuxhaven, through the canal to Keil, back to Holland, Den Helder, then Newcastle and to Immingham where we assumed duties as Royal Yacht Guard Ship, up the east coast with the Queen. She did a tour of the Kingdom of Fife by road from Rosyth to the Tay, relaxation in Dundee, and round the top of Scotland to Pompey. En route we spent three weeks around the Clyde estuary; Greenock, Garloch,

Rothsey, Ardrishaig, Lochgilphead, Inverary. A nice trip.

Incidentally, should you ever whilst in Germany be invited by the German navy to a beer and schnapps party, think twice about accepting unless you have a very strong stomach. We had this experience in Cuxhaven. On arrival at their base, we went to a first floor room and as soon as we were seated, waitresses came in and put out two glasses for each person; one beer, one spirit. Both glasses were filled to the brim, the mess President made a short welcoming speech and the serious business began. He downed the schnapps in one throw, followed immediately by the beer. The assembled company followed suit. Waitresses were recalled and glasses recharged. One of our number made a short speech in reply, and the ritual was repeated. Waitresses recalled, glasses recharged. Need I go on? Round followed round, then came the inevitable German drinking songs; first chorus on the floor, second chorus standing on the chairs, third chorus standing on the tables. Thank goodness the chandeliers were high.

At one stage during the evening I had to go and find a door marked 'Herren'. On emerging I discovered an outside door and decided a lungful of fresh air would not be amiss. I was just about to take the third lungful when two big Germans, and I mean big, came up either side of me and directed me back upstairs, saying, 'You are vasting drinkink time!' So back upstairs we went. Come the dawn! No further comment necessary! But we later decided that having accepted their hospitality we were obliged to reciprocate. The facilities just did not exist on a destroyer to stage a similar do so we decided to ask them to stage it and we would foot the bill. The whole procedure was duplicated forty-eight hours later. I have a headache every time I think about it!

I must record one incident here. Whilst at Ardrishaig, four of us set off up the side of the loch to Lochgilphead, a change of scenery really. It was further than we anticipated and we were getting a bit foot weary when a car stopped and gave us a lift. When we arrived the driver said, 'How are you going to return?' and gave us his phone number saying he would pick us up and return us to Ardrishaig. We had no thought of imposing further on his generosity, but at the end of the evening the thought of that long walk back changed our minds. We phoned him after some soul searching and he got out of bed and took us back to the ship. He wouldn't hear of a word of thanks. He turned out to be the local dentist. Perhaps he thought he owed humanity something.

These aforementioned one-and-a-half year commissions were designed to spend half abroad and half in home waters. A good idea. So our next stint of the commission was to be the Med. – an old stamping ground for me.

We left the UK with a new crew, always uneasy days whilst people find their feet. A week or so was spent around Portland, a 'working up period', then off to Gibraltar and Malta and down to business. The Cyprus trouble was at its height by now and we were soon off there.

Our role was once again in support of the army and consisted mainly of maintaining a sea blockade of the island to stop men and munitions getting to the rebels; also to stop wanted men getting out. We were not over-popular with the law abiding Greek fishermen plying their legitimate trade around the coast.

To be stopped and have your boat searched by the navy could take hours, and that was hours out of a working day when you should have been earning a living. But such are the penalties to be paid in such a campaign. For us it was a tedious unrewarding job rather than an action-packed one. I have always got along well with Greeks and Turks and wished they could get along better with one another. To suddenly find that the former (or some of them anyway) would wish to blow me sky high or stab me in the back, I found thoroughly distasteful. But there it was.

We visited Limmasol, Paphos, Larnaca, Famagusta and Kyrenia. I quite enjoyed Famagusta, particularly the old Turkish quarter, and Kyrenia must surely be the loveliest spot on the island. But you don't appreciate beauty so much with a revolver at your waist and looking over your shoulder constantly.

We dropped anchor one dark winter's night just off Paphos, and no sooner had we done so than we received a lamp signal from the shore, inviting several of us, by rank, to a trip ashore and a few drinks. We knew army units were nearby, but was this a trap? This was rebel hot-bed territory. Very unsure of our ground, we landed on a deserted beach and crept ashore, guns in hand. We needn't have worried; it was the army that greeted us and led us to their camp. It was the Black Watch, and the date 30 December, one night before Hogmanay.

They were so glad to see us they promptly advanced Hogmanay by twenty-four hours. It was a night to remember, and in the small hours we crept back to our boat, watched over by the army, of course, and back aboard.

One night among many such with the army in different parts of the world. Another took place in Famagusta with my old friends from Far East days, the Royal Ulster Rifles. I renewed a few acquaintances from those days including the one who painted the Welsh regimental mascot green in Hong Kong. Shhh!

We managed a bit of a break on one occasion between Cyprus patrols, a few days in Beirut. Imagine going to Beirut for a break from a conflict area. But the Lebanon was a different place from the war-torn wreckage it is today. I even managed a road trip down the coast to Sidon and one into the Shouff mountains. I met up with some Canadian soldiers here, on leave from the UN force in Israel's Gaza Strip. Great guys, they knew their way around and I was able to benefit from their experience.

But generally speaking we did not get many breaks during these twelve months; it was all go. The entire Med. fleet at this time consisted of five destroyers and some minesweepers. Fine until the Cyprus situation tied them down for most of their time. We still had NATO commitments and quite often we would leave Cyprus and tear from one end of the Med. to the other to take part in an exercise in mid-Atlantic and back again. None of our North Atlantic allies had this burden. But we did it. We always kept our end up. It took its toll on men and ships eventually. Ships were run into the ground, metaphorically speaking that is, through lack of maintenance. When we did get alongside somewhere, men were in need of a break and a lot of routine maintenance went by the board.

On one of these Atlantic exercises, *Armada* contacted condenser-itis, which any marine engineer will tell you is pretty serious. The UK force was just three destroyers and had we dropped out it would have constituted a one third reduction in our force. We could imagine some of our allies pointing the finger and inferring inefficiency. We couldn't have that so we struggled on, worked night and day and finished the exercise. We limped into Gibraltar on conclusion and spent the next five days working day and night with dockyard help, correcting the fault and preparing for sea again. That five days was right over an Easter weekend.

Even over the Christmas of that year, when we were due for a break, it went wrong. We docked in mid-December in Malta, and a few of us decided to take advantage of this to bring our families out from the UK to spend Christmas together. My family had not had a holiday that year because I was away and would not get one the following summer for the very same reason, so I figured that a week or so in Malta would do them all good. They duly arrived and we had a few days together. Then the bottom dropped out of that world. The destroyer that had relieved us in Cyprus became involved in a collision and was damaged. *Armada* had to undock and head eastwards again, arriving 23 December. I had to leave the family in Malta to get home as best they could. They made it, arriving in the UK on 24 December. See what I mean by all 'go'?

Having said all that, having had a moan, there were highlights to the year, as a list of ports of call and places visited will indicate – Tunis, Marseille, Toulon, Perpignan, Gulf Juan, Naples, Barcelona, Sardinia, Athens and Istanbul. There were others but that will do to be getting on with. One end of the Med. to the other and a few different cultures. Time in any of them was not long, a few days usually; some were in connection with allied exercises, briefing and de-briefing and a few days' break after an arduous exercise, all interspersed with duties in Cyprus.

I met some very interesting people from time to time in various circumstances. One such in Toulon was a French matelot who I sought direction from in the street when trying to find Toulon railway station. He took me to the station and on making enquiries as to train times, found nothing suitable and suggested I travel by coach. He then took me to the coach station, booked my seat and then, finding we had time to spare, took me for a drink and told me his story. He was in fact a Russian who had defected some years previously and had fought for France in Vietnam against communism. A most interesting character. Our whole association took only a couple of hours but he was one of the episodes in life that linger long.

Another such meeting occurred in Tunis. We were only there for three nights. The first night I went ashore after our training stint and got attacked by a 'friendly' Arab with a knife. Well it was a goodwill visit after all. The next day I met a gentleman and wife, an English couple, who took me on a tour of the area, visiting Carthage and other places of interest, finishing up at Sidi-bou-Said for dinner. Then back to their villa at Hannibal's Harbour (where the elephants were embarked for the European expedition). I stayed the night with them and he returned me to the ship in the morning. Hospitality such as that is really appreciated, believe me.

Incidentally, the knife wielding Arab came unstuck. He picked the wrong lad to mug. I was totally fit at the time and he came off second best in the struggle.

There was a humorous touch on one occasion in Malta. We landed on Manoel Island, where the navy had large sports facilities, to find an athletic track marked out. An ideal opportunity, we thought, to check just how fit we were. We did four laps, checked the stop watch and found we had done our mile in about 4.10 minutes. Four minute miles were the exception rather than the rule and the world record was about three minutes fifty-eight seconds, so we congratulated ourselves; pretty good for a pair of old hacks. But prematurely I am afraid; a PTI came out of the pavilion to inform us that the track was only 400 yards, not 440 yards. That made our mile worth about five minutes. Ah well!

Possibly the most influential visits of our time in the Med. were the last ones, to Athens and Istanbul. When the cease-fire was signed in Cyprus, someone in Whitehall decided that it would be a good idea to send a naval presence to Greece and Turkey to attempt to mend fences; to repair Anglo-Greek and Anglo-Turkish relationships at grass roots level.

The difference between cease-fire and ceasing hostilities was vast. In fact hostilities went on for years, but I suppose the thinking was right. And who got the job? *Armada!* We were already in the area anyway, so that did influence the decision, I guess. Whitehall stipulated that it had to be a picked crew. What that amounted to in fact was not allowing known trouble makers ashore. The 'Jolly Jack' who was prone to trouble under the influence of drink would be kept aboard. The formula had worked for years, and was implemented on this occasion.

When we were assigned this task, our hearts went down. The three communities, British/Greek/Turkish, had been at loggerheads for so long in this area; and there we were being chucked in at the deep end, as we saw it. I could see no way we could win or even draw.

But in the event it worked out wonderfully well. That idiot in Whitehall who thought up the idea was not such an idiot after all. We received a great reception in both capitals. The English communities played a big part in this, through their associations. The foundations were already laid prior to arrival.

Firstly Istanbul for seven days. The British community had hired a disused theatre and set up a sort of HQ for us, a centre from which to operate with a bar and snack facilities, all at subsidized prices. It was my first visit to Turkey and I enjoyed it.

The British Embassy had a club for its staff there, in the grounds of the embassy; very well appointed, as one would imagine, and we were invited to partake of the facilities during the visit. I thoroughly enjoyed my visits there and met some nice people. There was a sequel to this. Many years later I was standing at a bar in Cambridge with only one other person doing likewise. I thought to myself, 'I know that guy.' He was looking at me and thinking the same and after a spell we got into conversation to find that our previous encounter had been in the Embassy Club in Istanbul. Ten years had elapsed but we recognized one another.

So to Athens. The British community had a club there, in permanent premises and they laid on a do for us one evening which was enjoyed by both sides.

A tour of the antiquities was arranged for us by the embassy and what more interesting antiquities are there than the ones in Athens? Our guide was an ex-lieutenant in the Greek Navy who had been civilianized in order to continue his archaeological studies. He was a man who really knew what he was talking about, compared to the usual tourist guides. I had been to Athens before, admittedly under very adverse circumstances in 1941, but I really learned a bit about it this time.

It was during this tour, as we passed the modern Olympic stadium, that my training partner asked if he could drop off and run a lap of the track. Permission was sought and granted. My friend had brought a track suit in anticipation so he changed and did the lap, purely for the honour of doing so. I must confess I opted out of that one.

I like to think we did our bit for British diplomacy on those two visits. I would go further. I firmly believe that if people could get together at that level, and understand one another's problems instead of leaving it to the politicians, that there would be a lot less tension in the world – a lot less need for military action. A lot less bloodshed. Homespun philosophy, yes, but true nevertheless.

There was one more task that fell to us before returning home; well it was on the way home actually. We had left Malta, called in at Gibraltar, and were heading north, going home again after a year away, when we were told we had to spend a week in Corruna on Cape Finistere. This was considered bad news at the time, our homecoming delayed by another week.

The reason for this diversion was to represent Britain in the celebrations to commemorate the battle of Corruna in which Anglo/Spanish forces had vanquished the French. This was the 150th anniversary of the battle, a really big one in Spanish history. They had requested units from the regiments that had actually participated in the hostilities, such as the Grenadier Guards amongst others. We were to represent the navy. The whole town was in fiesta for the week, dancing in the streets, fireworks, bull fights every afternoon, culminating in a big military parade on the Sunday through the town and to the tomb of General Moore, who is still revered in this part of Spain.

There was speculation among us as to how our lads would shape up on the parade in comparison to Guards regiments. A daunting prospect, but they need not have worried, they looked great. A well drilled squad of sailors, in full rig, white belts and gaiters, can compare with anyone. There is something of a swing to their marching, which compares favourably with the more stiff and formal gait of top soldiering. The Spanish crowds appreciated them anyway.

I saw quite a few bull fights here and got to appreciate them more because I understood them. I met up with a gentleman who was the chief tax official for the state of Galicia. Normally I have an aversion to such people, but I went to the correidas with him and his family, and they provided my education. Altogether a most enjoyable week and the fact that we were delayed on our return was soon forgotten.

This Atlantic coast of Spain is so different from the Med. coast; the 'Costas', the people, are so different too.

And so to Pompey again; some well enjoyed leave, a few repairs (ship not crew) and we were ready for the off again.

☆ ☆ ☆

For most of my time in the Service, if there had been trouble in the world in which my country was involved, I had been there. So why should it be any different now? The so-called Cod War was the next issue. It was all a bit unnecessary with the advantage of hindsight, but there it was. British fishermen were entitled to protection going about their legitimate pursuits. But the effect on me personally was that what should have been a relatively easy spell in home waters became a long hard slog. I think about forty per cent of the following year was spent in Icelandic waters.

Climatic conditions were atrocious most of the time. How trawlers managed to catch fish in those conditions constantly amazed me, but they did, and if there is one positive thought to come out of it all, it was admiration for Icelandic seamanship. They handled those ships in those conditions as easily as kids on skateboards in a local park.

Our tours of duty up there were about three weeks at a time. How many tours we did I can't remember, but I do recall that they were not exactly looked forward to. We were always glad when they were concluded and we went off to other duties.

The routine followed was this: the destroyer would set up an 'area' and all trawlers would be informed of the parameters of this area. If they chose to fish within them they would be under our protection. Some would of course choose not to, and then scream blue murder if the Icelanders harassed them, cut their trawls or whatever.

Generally the system worked well, but on some occasions

two Icelandic gunboats would attack at opposite ends of the area and we would have to hare from one incident to the other. It made life difficult to say the least but I think in the main we did the job we were there for reasonably well.

The later Cod Wars took place after I left the navy so I don't know much about them, but according to the press, they got more and more vicious. We had to retreat gracefully at the end.

We got along pretty well with the trawler crews. We would often be able to help them out technically when they broke down, and quite often different trawlers would send us over a sack of fish, beautiful fresh fish. It made me realize what a load of rubbish we purchase in shops and restaurants at home. The trawler owners were quite appreciative too, they would send us boxes of fresh fruit and vegetables. This plus the fish, really went down well, as frequently food was a bit short.

One trawler we struck up a good relationship with was the *Red Falcon* out of Fleetwood. Her radio operator was a bit of a wag, an amateur poet to boot. On many quiet evenings he would radio his humour to us; our operator would record same and relay it to us. It helped to pass the tedious hours and anything that did that was welcome. We were shattered when the news arrived that the *Red Falcon* had been lost, whilst returning to the UK from Iceland. She had run into bad weather and just disappeared. No radio message, no wreckage ever found, I understand. Just gone from the face of the earth. We felt we had lost an old friend. Such is the comradeship of the sea.

An appeal fund was launched by the Mayor of Fleetwood for dependents. We sent a letter off with our contribution. The whip-round among our crew produced a considerable amount of money for the fund – further evidence of the generosity of the matelot if the cause is good, and there is no better cause in his mind than the needs of dependents of old friends in trouble.

As a result of this liaison between *Armada* and the town of Fleetwood, the mayor wrote to the Admiralty requesting that we call in there some time so that the residents could show us due appreciation. Approval was given by our lords and masters and we were really looking forward to the visit. But almost on the eve of same, fate intervened, as it has a habit of doing. One of our turbo-forced draught fans in a boiler room failed to govern, went out of control and disintegrated. One boiler room out of action. We had to drop everything and make for Portsmouth on one boiler. We were lucky to avoid fatalities when this occurred and very sad to miss our Fleetwood visit.

Our Icelandic tours were interspersed with other duties, many and various. One such was another NATO scheme, held annually in northern Norway in which troops got the opportunity to train under arctic conditions.

Armada's contribution was to pick up a load of paratroops at Rosyth, across the North Sea, and unload them at Trondheim. They were then dropped by air into the Arctic Circle and carried out a mock battle whilst living off the land. The implications of that last sentence are, well, not easily absorbable. Living off the land in those conditions is unimaginable to most of us. But there you are, they may have to do that under real combat conditions one day. The experience would be invaluable.

Whilst they were so occupied we, the naval part of the force, carried out a mock battle around and in and out of the Lofoten Islands. A soft touch compared with the army's role. We won our battle actually. We managed a few trips ashore in the islands, purely recreational, but what a beautiful part of the world. Uninhabited just as nature made them. As previously said, I like Norway.

On completion of the exercise we picked up the troops and returned them to Rosyth. I well remember them walking up our gangway in Trondheim, collapsing and sleeping for hours on a steel deck in freezing temperatures. They were 'out' and happy to sleep just where they fell. One way and another, as the result of many experiences, as you may have perceived, I have a lot of respect for the British army.

Another duty that came our way, a less arduous one this time, was a goodwill visit to Bremen, Bremerhaven and Hamburg. Bremen was the centre piece to the trip. I enjoyed the trip as a whole; it was leisurely after our other duties and I remember some evenings ashore in good company. And why not?

Ports of call in the UK during this time included Invergordon, Scapa Flow, Buckie, Lough Foyle, Greenock,

Gourock, Gareloch and Rosyth. As will be noted, they were all northern ports, due of course to our primary area of operations being Iceland. We rarely came south at all, only for leave. Not that I am complaining. I took advantage of time in the Forth and Clyde areas to visit Edinburgh and Glasgow. I have always been happy in both areas.

So drew to a conclusion my final commission. Due to the accident in one boiler room, previously mentioned, it was decided not to re-commission *Armada*. She was to be put into reserve, a process taking three months. We carried this out in Portsmouth and handed her over to the dockyard. Always a sad affair to me, the demise of a good ship.

I heard subsequently that after laying in reserve for some time, she went to the great dockyard in the sky. More razor blades!

With only about twelve months to do to complete my time and be put out to grass, there was not enough time for another commission, so I finished up on HMS *Mull of Kintyre*. She was a minesweeper depot ship, undergoing an extended refit in Portsmouth dockyard. Ah! I thought, a nice quiet little backwater in which to finish my days. But it didn't work out that way; she was promptly brought forward to category A and the refit accelerated. However, I was still relieved before she sailed, due to my impending release. I was glad of that, otherwise it would have been back to the Med. again. I had served a total of seven years there, and reckoned it did not have much left to teach me.

So that's about it really. As I said at the outset, 'Great oaks from little acorns grow.' In twenty-two years I felt I had grown from a little acorn into as great an oak as I was ever going to be.

I served nearly ten of those years during some form of conflict. Another small statistic: out of twenty-two Christmases, I think I had four with my family.

Regrets, I had a few, but then again too few to mention.

6

Epilogue

There cannot be too many stories written in which the epilogue spans a longer period of years than the main story. But this is one such.

There is no prologue for the simple reason there is little to relate. I went to school, left school at fourteen and went to work. The main part of my life, the interesting part, the action filled part, the drama packed part, has been told in the foregoing, covering twenty-two years. The part following that, this part, has been ongoing for twenty-eight years. How many that will be extended by, well, who knows? Most of it has not been mundane, but mundane by comparison to the previous years. There have been many episodes worth recalling and worth recording, so I will confine the ongoing to a rough coverage of the whole interspersed with highlights that I think are worth telling.

I 'came ashore' late in 1961 and took an appointment as engineer in charge of a hospital in Cambridge. We moved to the village of Histon and there we stayed for seven-and-a-half years. I was promoted after a while and finished up as chief engineer of three hospitals. I missed the navy, of course I did, there is no use denying it. I missed the way of life, the comradeship, the *esprit-de-corps*. I soon found that it did not exist in civilian life, at least not to the extent I was used to. But the adjustment had to be made, and made it was. But it took time.

I missed the constant change of horizon. But I did tell the family that I did not hanker after holidays abroad, certainly not the Med. The thought of the emerging 'Costas' appalled me. But on looking around I realized that although I had seen most of the world, there were a few gaps on my doorstep. North Wales, the Yorkshire Moors, the Lake District. So for the next few holidays, those gaps were filled and I enjoyed them. We would put our two daughters in the back of the car and set off for a predetermined area, staying B and B; and if we liked it, stayed for a bit, if not, moved on to the next place. We saw a lot of the country that way.

This period coincided with my final demise from the boxing world. Well, officially that is. I have done a bit of helping and advising since then, but that is all. On entering civilian circles I had to register as a referee with the county association. The local club in Cambridge made my application to register, but their secretary told me from the outset that I wouldn't be accepted as the county association was dominated by the university and I did not have a degree. I couldn't believe my ears, but so it was; they did not even acknowledge my application.

At that time there was such a dearth of qualified officials that tournaments were having to be cancelled all over the country. Now there was yours truly, fully qualified, and with more experience than any of their referees, refused due to academic bigotry.

So I walked away from the scene with a shrug. I figured it was their loss rather than mine.

After seven-and-a-half years in Cambridge I decided it was time to move on, so I applied for a similar appointment elsewhere. Almost immediately I realized I had made an error of judgment. Most of the major decisions of my life have been well made, but I certainly fell over with this one. I don't make much criticism of nursing or medical staff, indeed in recent years they have cut me open and stitched me up on not a few occasions, but if ever anywhere there was a more bumbling, lunatic set of administrators I hope I never meet them. After six months, during which I nearly took leave of my sanity, I resigned and moved on again.

For the next couple of years I did all sorts of things, mostly self-employed. I was a works engineer in the diamond industry, a maintenance supervisor, a property surveyor, a planned preventative maintenance consultant. You name it!

Then, career wise, I settled down again and became a

quality control/assurance inspector with the water division of a large international engineering company. This was my forte; they were a good company and I stayed there until retirement (early) in 1981. The variety of work environs was infinite: power stations, refineries, petrochemical generally and municipal works. I was my own boss, made my decisions and travelled to every corner of the United Kingdom and beyond, by company car and plane.

But there is always a price to pay and into my sixties I began to find the travelling a strain, driving in London, Manchester and Birmingham. There was no enjoyment in it any more, so I decided on early retirement before my judgment became impaired.

Having got over my 'not wanting to go abroad' period by this time, we started to travel again on holidays. It started with a four day trip to Moscow then, when we discussed holidays the next year, my wife again wanted to go abroad. That started a long run which continues until today, often twice a year. A list of places visited will, I think, suffice to show the extent of our travels: Austria, Italy (2), Russia, Romania, Greece, Crete, Turkey, Spain (2), France (5), Andorra, Norway, Holland, Belgium, Germany, Morocco, Portugal, Hungary, Yugoslavia (2). Most times we toured the country rather than stay in one town or resort.

Highlights? There were many but I would like to recall a few.

Whilst walking along a mountain track high in the Carpathians, above Brasov in Romania, we saw way ahead of us along the track, a woman with a child picking wild flowers. The child, a little girl suddenly ran back towards us and presented Mary with a bunch of wild blooms, curtsied sweetly, and ran back to her mother. Not a word was spoken. But could any spoken word have enhanced the situation?

Whilst on tour in Morocco, we stopped at a small village for lunch one day, and whilst waiting we wandered in the hotel's extensive gardens and admired the roses. The head gardener, seeing our interest, picked one of his prize blooms and presented it to my wife with due flourish. Little things, a flower, a few flowers, but they mean a lot and linger in the memory.

Whilst in Budapest, we went to dinner one night in one of

the underground restaurants in old Buda. Not just underground restaurants, they are several storeys underground. The leader of the inevitable gypsy orchestra picked one female to serenade from amongst the diners. He picked Mary that night and her day was made.

A similar experience came my way in Romania, when the girl cabaret singer singled me out for attention.

We stayed for a few days once in a little village in Greece, on the Peloponese, a delightful little place. We got into conversation with the hotel owner on the first night. He proudly told us that he had been to London twice, and had we been to Greece before?

I said, 'Yes, I was here in 1941 and 1958.'

'That's not possible, the Germans were here in 1941,' he replied.

'Don't tell me mate,' was the answer that came to mind, but I did not express it.

The conversation continued, and when it was revealed that I had fought in the battles for Greece and Crete, he told my wife, 'That man is a bloody hero. Any man that fought in those battles in the Royal Navy is a bloody hero.' It is appropriate here to remember that Crete was never invaded by sea, only by air. He was a Cretan. The outcome of that conversation was that I was treated with due reverence by the hotel staff for the rest of the stay. When I entered the dining room, a waiter would dash up and pull my chair out, only mine, not the wife's. After all it was me who was the hero, I told her.

The word must have been passed through the village for the reverence extended there. Once again not a word was spoken on either side, but was one necessary?

Crete brought back more memories for me. I admired the fierce independence of the mountain people and their patriotism. This has been lost to a certain extent in the coastal areas with the advent of tourism. A pity. But, all in all, I admired the Cretans. In the mountains I found that they rather loved us Brits but would not countenance the Germans. But money talked in the resorts and Germans were accepted.

A rather similar situation existed in Yugoslavia. Our second holiday there was a wine tour of Slovenia. A lovely trip, well, what I remember of it! The attitude of the people here was akin to the Cretans, whereas in the resorts on the coast it was vastly different.

An emotional spot for me in Yugoslavia was the Franja Hospital. It is a museum/memorial now, but its origins should not be forgotten. It was the partisan hospital during the war, hidden deep in a gorge. The Germans never discovered it. Any description I could give of it here would be totally inadequate; it really has to be seen to be appreciated.

When the Falkland crisis boiled up, we happened to be in Lisbon, and I found it difficult to obtain any information whatsoever as to what was happening. I was worried to death. How could they possibly manage in a war situation without me? Eventually I convinced myself that they would be all right. 'Sit down you silly old fool,' I told myself. By then I would have been more of a hindrance than a help and, as events proved, they did manage without me; rather well I thought.

On a business trip to Eire, one of many, whilst staying in Cork I got into conversation with Lord Longford, who was staying at the same hotel, prior to a recorded interview for Radio Cork. He went off to deliver a lecture to a convocation of bishops and I immediately met an English business man from Dublin. He was an old soldier who had fought in Greece, been rescued by HMS *Kelly*, Lord Mountbatten's ship, and then ultimately rescued by the *Naiad*. He said he owed his life to the navy and now was the time to settle up. It turned out to be quite a night, one way and another.

One more of life's interesting and amusing incidents; it was about my becoming a Lord! Through the Institute of Hospital Engineering (of which I was a member) I went to dinner in the Houses of Parliament as guest of Patrick Jenkin, then the member for Woodford. On arrival I was shown into a reception room, with a bar in one corner. I looked around at the few guests already there; no one I knew, so I got myself a whisky and soda and wandered over to the window and looked out over the river. It was a nice summer evening and the windows were open. As I stood there, a river boat full of tourists cruised slowly by, all looking up at the House. One lady, seeing me at the window, gave me a wave. I raised my glass in acknowledgement. She then announced loudly in American to the rest of the passengers, 'Gee, that must have been a real English Lord.' They all waved to me then. I gave them the best imitation I could muster of a 'royal' wave, glass of whisky in hand.

I was fortunate after retirement to be offered several 'jobs' from time to time. They kept me occupied, kept the brain ticking over, as it were. I did a few consultancy jobs for my old company, work that was not completed when I left. I carried on until contracts were finalized. Some other companies that had worked for us also made use of my services and I took that as a compliment.

Then I did a year at the British Engineerium as instructor/lecturer to their juniors a couple of days a week. I found that interesting and rewarding – mentally and morally, if not financially.

> The final curtain! Well, so far.
> I did what I had to do,
> and saw it through
> and I never whinged.